HELLO MUDDAH, HELLO FADDUH!

The Allan Sherman Musical

Conceived and Written
by
Douglas Bernstein & Rob Krausz

Hello Muddah, Hello Fadduh! **received 4 Drama Desk Nominations, and the Outer Critics' Circle Nomination for Outstanding Off-Broadway Musical.**

SAMUEL FRENCH, INC.
45 West 25th Street NEW YORK 10010
7623 Sunset Boulevard HOLLYWOOD 90046
LONDON TORONTO

Printed in the U.S.A.
ISBN 0 573 69467-2

Special thanks to Robert Sherman, Nancy Sherman, Albert Hague, Mark Edelman/Theatre League and Jennifer Manocherian.

To my mother — for writing me everyday at camp, and my father — for being the funniest writer I know.

—D.B.

To Alex and Ida — my muddah and fadduh, my sistuh, Diane, her hubbuh, David, and my beautiful niecuhs, Lucy and Sophie.

—R.K.

IMPORTANT BILLING AND CREDIT REQUIREMENTS

All producers of HELLO MUDDAH, HELLO FADDUH! *must* give credit to the Authors of the Work in all programs distributed in connection with performances of the Work, and in all instances in which the title of the Work appears for the purposes of advertising, publicizing or otherwise exploiting a production thereof; including, without limitation, all programs, souvenir books and playbills. The names of the Authors *must* also appear on a separate line in which no other matter appears, immediately following the title of the Work, and *must* be in size of type not less than 50% of the size of type used for the title of the Work. Billing *must* be substantially as follows:

(Name of Producer)

presents

HELLO MUDDAH, HELLO FADDUH!

The Allan Sherman Musical

Conceived and Written by

Douglas Bernstein and Rob Krausz

HELLO MUDDAH, HELLO FADDUH! was presented by Diane F. Krausz, Jennifer A. Manocherian and David A. Blumberg, at Circle in the Square Theatre in New York City. It premiered on December 5, 1992. The cast included:

Stephen Berger.................................. Man 2
Tovah Feldshuh.......................... Woman 2
Jason Graae .... Man 1
Paul Kreppel .... Man 3
Mary Testa................................ Woman 1

Setting by Michael Downs
Lighting by Howard Werner
Costumes by Susan Branch
Sound by Tom Morse
Musical Direction and Vocal Arrangements by David Evans
Orchestrations by David Lawrence
Production Stage Manager: R. Wade Jackson
Additional Music by Albert Hague

Entire Production Directed and Choreographed by Michael Leeds

MUSICAL NUMBERS

ACT I

1. OVERTURE

Prologue:

2. OPENING GOULASH.................................... The Company

Scene 1: He is Born

3. BARRY .... The Company
3A. Hebraic Organ Music
4. SARAH JACKMAN .... Barry, Sarah
4A. Scene Change 1

Scene 2: He Learns

5. WON'T YOU COME HOME, DISRAELI?........... Sarah, Louise
6. SIR GREENBAUM'S MADRIGAL .... Barry, Morty
7. GOOD ADVICE................................ Kalodner and Company
7A. GOOD ADVICE - Playoff

Scene 3: He Leaves Home

7B. Cha-Cha
8. I CAN'T DANCE... Barry, Carlotta
9. KISS OF MYER .... Myer, Carlotta, Sarah
10. HELLO MUDDAH, HELLO FADDUH! .... Barry
10A. Scene Change 2

Scene 4: He Grows Up

10B. Pomp and Circumstance
11. NO ONE'S PERFECT .... The Company
11A. Scene Change 3
12. ONE HIPPOPOTAMI...................................... Barry, Sarah

Scene 5: He is Wed

12A. Samba
12B. Buffet Fanfare
13. PHIL MEDLEY .... Phil
13A. PHIL - Playoff
13B. Wedding March
14. HARVEY AND SHEILA.............................. Harvey, Sheila, and Company

ACT II

15. ENTR'ACTE

Scene 6: He Reproduces

16. ROBBIE .... The Company
17. SHAKE HANDS WITH YOUR UNCLE MAX .. The Company

Scene 7: He Moves

18. HERE'S TO THE CRABGRASS .... Barry, Sarah
19. SHINE ON, HARVEY BLOOM .... Mr. Bloom and Company
20. MEXICAN HAT DANCE....................... Sheila and Company
21. GROW, MRS. GOLDFARB .... Goldfarb
21A. Scene Change 4
22. JUMP DOWN, SPIN AROUND .... Store Manager and Company
22A. JUMP DOWN - Playoff

Scene 8: He is Older

23. CRAZY DOWNTOWN..................................... Sarah, Barry
24. DID I EVER REALLY LIVE?* .... Barry
24A. HELLO MUDDAH, HELLO FADDUH! - Reprise.......... Phil
25. LIKE YOURS*... Barry, Sarah
25A. Scene Change 5

Scene 9: He is Old

26. DOWN THE DRAIN*................................ Nat, Doris, Lenny
27. THE BALLAD OF HARRY LEWIS................. The Company
28. Bows

Epilogue: They Medley

29. MEDLEY .... The Company
30. Exit Music

*Music by Albert Hague

CHARACTER BREAKDOWN

MAN 1

Characters:

Prologue: -- Intern/Nun/Baby
Act I and II: -- Barry
Act II, Sc. 7: -- Rose

MAN 2

Characters:

Prologue: -- Doctor
Act I, Sc. 1: -- Mohel
Sc. 2: -- Morty
Sc. 3: -- Myer
Sc. 4: -- Choir
Sc. 5: -- Phil

Act II, Sc. 6: -- Robbie
Sc. 7: ---------------------------- Mr. Bloom, Store Clerk
Sc. 8: -- Policeman
Sc. 9: -- Lenny

MAN 3

Characters:

Prologue -- Father
Act I, Sc. 2: -- Mr. Kalodner
Sc. 3: -- Leonard
Sc. 4: -- Principal
Sc. 5: -- Harvey

Act II, Sc. 6: -- Harvey
Sc. 7: -- Goldfarb, Shirley
Sc. 8: -- Boyfriend
Sc. 9: -- Nat

WOMAN 1

Characters:

Prologue: --Nurse
Act I and II: --Sarah

WOMAN 2

Characters:

Prologue:		---Mother
Act I,	Sc. 2:	-- Louise
	Sc. 3:	--- Esther, Carlotta
	Sc. 4:	---Choir
	Sc. 5:	-- Sheila
Act II,	Sc. 6:	-- Sheila
	Sc. 7:	-- Sheila
	Sc. 8:	---Sophie
	Sc. 9:	---Doris

HELLO MUDDAH, HELLO FADDUH!

ACT I

Prologue

(As the audience enters, a slide is projected onto a screen upstage. It reads: "HELLO MUDDAH, HELLO FADDUH!"

The set, and indeed the theater wall itself, is made up of enlarged photographs, postcards, letters, greeting cards, telegrams, and formal announcements documenting various moments in the life of our mythical hero, Barry Bockman.

A small MUSICAL ENSEMBLE is seated upstage. The band is basically the group that you'd see at any self-respecting Bar Mitzvah.

[Music Cue #1: OVERTURE]

The pre-set fades out, and the BAND plays an incredibly majestic version of the song, "Hello Muddah, Hello Fadduh!" complete with powerful, angelic VOICES.

When the piece reaches a climax, we hear in the silence: a WOMAN MOANING. The MUSIC continues; the WOMAN moans in rhythm.

LIGHTS UP on a birth in progress — the DOCTOR stands between the legs of a PREGNANT WOMAN lying, head downstage, on a bed. An INTERN and a NURSE are assisting, while a very NERVOUS FATHER-TO-BE looks on anxiously.

The DOCTOR notices the presence of the audience first, and begins to sing.)

[Music Cue #2: OPENING GOULASH]

(Brahms: "Hungarian Dance #5")

DOCTOR.
IF YOU LIKE A MUSICAL REVUE
WE WILL—
NURSE.
—DELIVER
DOCTOR/NURSE.
A LITTLE ONE FOR YOU!
INTERN.
SOON YOU WILL KNOW WHAT THIS SHOW IS ABOUT
FATHER-TO-BE.
STICK AROUND YOU'LL WANNA SEE HOW EV'RYTHING COMES OUT
MOTHER. (*Joining in fervidly.*)
HEY!
ALL.
WE WILL SING GREAT MUSIC

(MOTHER moans.)

FATHER.
OH, THE NOISE WE'RE GONNA MAKE
ALL.
WE HAVE SUCH SURPRISES
MOTHER. (*Offering a piece.*)
LOOK, I BROUGHT A LITTLE CAKE
INTERN/NURSE.
WE'LL HAVE PASSION AND ROMANCE
DOCTOR.
A LITTLE DANCE, A LITTLE SONG
ALL.
AND THE BEST NEWS—
FATHER.
THE WHOLE THING ISN'T REALLY VERY LONG

ALL.
ALL THE MANY CHARACTERS YOU'LL SEE HERE
INTERN.
TEACHERS
DOCTOR.
LAWYERS
NURSE. (*Off Doctor.*)
AND A NICE M.D. HERE
FATHER.
LATER, MY ACCOUNTANT'S GONNA BE HERE
INTERN. (*Exiting.*)
DOC, I THINK WE NEED A NEW I.V. HERE
FATHER. (*Soft-shoeing.*)
MOTHERS-IN-LAW CONSTANTLY COMPLAINING
NURSE. (*Off Father.*)
RELATIVES WHO THINK THEY'RE ENTER-TAINING
DOCTOR.
WE'LL TAKE YOU TO BARBECUES AND BRISSES
ALL.
THAT'S THE KIND OF MUSICAL THAT THIS IS

(The MOTHER sits up with a struggle. SHE catches her breath, then begins to kick her legs and sing:)

MOTHER.
IN THE CAST—WE PUT ALL THESE FOLKS
ALL.
SHY SUMMER CAMPERS
SALESMEN WHO TELL JOKES
SWEET, BLUSHING BRIDES
THERE'S NO ONE WE MISS
YOU'LL SEE EVERY KIND OF THING—
WELL, EVERYTHING BUT *THIS*!

(A NUN jumps out.)

NUN.
HEY!

(NUN exits. Tambourines are pulled out.)

MOTHER.
THIS IS ONE MAN'S STORY
NURSE.
(WE MADE IT UP, BUT WHAT THE HECK)
MOTHER.
CALL HIM BARRY BOCKMAN
DOCTOR. (*Up from his examination.*)
HE'LL BE OUT IN JUST A SEC
MOTHER.
FROM HIS FIRST WORDS IN CHILDHOOD TO HIS GRADUATION SPEECH
OTHERS.
TO THE DAY HE ENDS UP DOWN IN MIAMI BEACH

(The MOTHER moans more seriously now but still in rhythm.)

ALL.
EVERY SCENE IS TOTALLY CHAOTIC
MOTHER.
EVERYONE IS BASICALLY NEUROTIC
ALL.
BUT WE HAVE AN AWFUL LOT OF FUN, TOO
LATER ON, WHO KNOWS, YOU'LL GET THE NUN, TOO

(NUN sticks "her" head out:)

NUN.
HEY! (*NUN exits.*)
ALL.
NOW IT'S TIME TO GET OFF OUR TUSH

BRING OUT THE HERO, TELL HIS STORY—

(The DOCTOR is handed a catcher's mitt:)

DOCTOR. *(To Mother.)*
PUSH!
ALL.
LIFE WAS BEGUN ON ONE EARLY MORN
THAT'S WHERE WE'LL START—
THE PART WHERE HE IS BORN!

(On the last beat, the BABY is revealed.)

BABY.
WAAH!

(A new SLIDE comes on the screen—the first of many that will announce the periods in Barry's life, and the sections of this show. It simply reads:)

HE IS BORN

(ALL but BARRY exit. As the LIGHTS come up, we hear:)

[Music Cue #3: BARRY]

("Mary's a Grand Old Name")

ALL. *(O.S.)*
WE'LL CALL HIM BARRY, BARRY
THAT'LL BE THE BABY'S NAME ...
BARRY. *(Out front.)* Hello, Muddah! Hello, Fadduh!

(Now, on tape, we hear the VOICES of ALL of BARRY's loving family and neighbors. BARRY reacts in turn to whatever is said:)

LOTS OF VOICES. Ohhhhh ... look! What a sweetheart!... Precious!... Those cheeks! Uh uh uh ... (*The BABY's cheeks are pulled.*)

MAN. Guess what I brought?! A savings bond.

MAN. I brought an Israeli Bond.

MAN. I brought James Bond!

WOMAN. Murray, you're such a kidder.

MAN. Oh ... He's got his father's eyes ...

WOMAN. He's got his mother's smile ...

(BARRY holds up a wooden foot.)

MAN. Hey! He's got his uncle's foot!

MOTHER. Our little boy. He looks so happy.

FATHER. Why not? He's a baby. What does he have to worry about?

[Music Cue #3A: HEBRAIC ORGAN MUSIC]

(The MOHEL enters, clearly identifiable by a giant gleaming pair of SCISSORS. BARRY's expression abruptly changes, and HE looks to the audience.)

BARRY. Uh-oh.

(The MOHEL sets up, and does his MOHEL routine.)

MOHEL. (*Holding up scissors.*) FORESKIN and seven years ago!... I'm kidding, I'm kidding ... Why do I do it?... For the TIPS, of course!... Heh heh ... Hey, I hate to CUT THIS SHORT ... (*Scissors fall shut precipitously.*) Ho!... but I got work to do!

(HE exits. We hear a PHONE RINGING ... somewhere. Confused for a moment, BARRY reaches down and pulls out a little blue baby telephone.)

BARRY. Hello?

(Another carriage appears—this one holds a BABY GIRL, SARAH. SHE is holding a pink baby telephone. MUSIC begins.)

[Music Cue #4: SARAH JACKMAN]

SARAH. Hello? Is this 418-9749?
BARRY. Sarah?
SARAH. Barry?
BARRY. (*Sings.*)

("Frère Jacques")

SARAH JACKMAN, SARAH JACKMAN
HOW'S BY YOU? HOW'S BY YOU?
HOW'S BY YOU THE FAMILY?
HOW'S YOUR SISTER EMILY?
SARAH.
SHE'S NICE, TOO
BARRY.
SHE'S NICE, TOO
SARAH.
BARRY BOCKMAN, BARRY BOCKMAN
SO WHAT'S NEW?
SO WHAT'S NEW?
HOW'S YOUR BROTHER BERNIE?
BARRY.
HE'S A BIG ATTORNEY
SARAH.
HE'S NICE, TOO
BARRY.
HE'S NICE, TOO

(THEY let themselves out of their respective carriages, and try out their walking.)

BARRY.
SARAH JACKMAN, SARAH JACKMAN
HOW'S BY YOU, HOW'S BY YOU?
HOW'S YOUR COUSIN LENA?
SARAH.
MOVED TO PASADENA
HOW'S YOUR SISTER DORIS?
BARRY.
STILL WITH WILLIAM MORRIS
HOW'S YOUR COUSIN SHIRLEY?
SARAH.
SHE GOT MARRIED EARLY
HOW'S YOUR BROTHER BENTLEY?
BARRY.
FEELING BETTER MENT'LLY
WHAT'S WITH UNCLE SIDNEY?
SARAH.
THEY TOOK OUT A KIDNEY
I AIN'T HEARD FROM SONYA
BARRY.
I'LL GET HER TO PHONE YA
HOW'S YOUR COUSIN MANNY?
SARAH.
WORKS FOR MANNY HANNY
HOW'S YOUR UNCLE NATHAN?
BARRY.
HIM I GOT NO FAITH IN
HOW'S HIS DAUGHTER RITA?
SARAH.
A REGULAR LOLITA
BARRY.
SHE'S NICE, TOO
SHE'S NICE, TOO

BARRY.	**SARAH.**
SARAH JACKMAN, SARAH JACKMAN	

HOW'S BY YOU, HOW'S BY YOU?	BARRY BOCKMAN, BARRY BOCKMAN
GIVE REGARDS TO HY NOW	SO WHAT'S NEW?
GOTTA SAY GOODBYE NOW	SO WHAT'S NEW?
TOOTALOO	GIVE REGARDS TO MOE NOW
TOOTALOO	WELL, I GOTTA GO NOW

BOTH.
TOOTALOO, TOOTALOO
TOO ... TALOO!

[Music Cue #4A: Scene Change 1]

(THEY hang up their phones. LIGHTS fade. CHANGE MUSIC takes us into:)

HE LEARNS

(A TEACHER stands in front of a slidescreen.
On a blackboard nearby: "TISHMAN ELEMENTARY SCHOOL. GRADE V: MR. KALODNER—HISTORY."
The bow-tied, scholarly, excitable TEACHER, MR. KALODNER, holds a clicker and uses a pointer.)

MR. KALODNER. Alright, class, settle down.

Now, children, you've reached the end of fifth grade, and I want to go over what the final History test will cover:

First, you'll be asked to identify important ancient architecture—*(HE clicks. SLIDE: CLEOPATRA'S NEEDLE.)* Cleopatra's Needle ... *(Clicks. SLIDE: PYRAMID.)* Cheops' Pyramid ... and ... *(Clicks.*

SLIDE: VEGAS HOTEL, circa late '50's, early '60's with funny marquee—"Tonight – Buddy Hackett and the Golddiggers", or whatever.) ... Caesar's Palace. There will be a multiple choice section on the *Canterbury Tales*, and the gifted author who wrote them ... (*HE clicks. SLIDE: A CANTOR.*) — Cantor Berry. Next, you'll be asked to identify famous people with their holidays. (*Clicks. SLIDE: COLUMBUS.*) Columbus Day. (*Clicks. SLIDE: WASHINGTON.*) Washington's Birthday. And, of course ... (*Clicks. SLIDE: Jack Webb in "Dragnet."*) Good Friday ...

Finally, there will be an essay on famed British statesman, Neville Chamberlain. (*SLIDE: NEVILLE CHAMBERLAIN.*) And his nephews—(*SLIDE: DR. KILDARE.*) Richard Chamberlain, and—(*SLIDE: WILT CHAMBERLAIN.*) Wilt. (*Several clicks. HE gestures:*) May I have the lights please, Morty? Lights, please.

(The LIGHTS come up, and the CLASS is revealed. There's SARAH, a cute, conservatively knee-socked eight-year-old, LOUISE, her friend, the teacher's pet, and BARRY, now also eight years old.)

MR. KALODNER. Now you all know your final reports are due today. Why don't we start with ...

(BARRY tries to hide. LOUISE raises her hand, dying to answer.)

MR. KALODNER. ... Louise, and Sarah.
SARAH. Oh, no ...

(SARAH gives Louise a dirty look, as THEY take center stage. Mild MARCHING MUSIC.)

[Music Cue #5: WON'T YOU COME HOME, DISRAELI?]

SARAH. (*Sings.*)
WHEN BENJAMIN DISRAELI WAS PRIME MINISTER OF ENGLAND
AND GOOD OLD QUEEN VICTORIA WAS THE QUEEN
LOUISE.
WHENEVER SHE WOULD NEED HIM FOR OFFICIAL PALACE BUSINESS
DISRAELI HE WAS NOWHERE TO BE SEEN
BOTH.
SHE WENT DOWN TO 10 DOWNING STREET
THE DOORBELL THERE SHE RANG

(THEY hear Big Ben CHIMES, and giggle.)

BOTH.
AND WHEN THERE WAS NO ANSWER
THIS IS WHAT THAT GOOD QUEEN ...

(THEY flip their reports over.)

BOTH.
... SANG

("Bill Bailey, Won't You Please Come Home?")

BOTH.
WON'T YOU COME HOME, DISRAELI?
WON'T YOU COME HOME?
COME HOME TO QUEEN VICTORIA
DON'T LEAVE THAT HOUSE OF COMMONS
AND THAT HOUSE OF LORDS
JUST SITTIN' WAITIN' FOR YA

YOU CLAIM OFFICIAL BUSINESS TOOK YOU AWAY
TO EGYPT AND BOMBAY AND ROME
NOW DON'T LEAVE ME FLAT

THE KEY TO THE PALACE IS UNDER THE MAT
DISRAELI, WON'T YOU PLEASE—

LOUISE. Take it, Sarah!

SARAH.
I MISS YOU, DIZZY!

BOTH.
DISRAELI, WON'T YOU PLEASE—

SARAH. Sing out, Louise!

LOUISE.
DON'T SAY YOU'RE BUSY

BOTH.
DISRAELI, WON'T YOU PLEASE COME HOME!?

The end.

(THEY pose.)

MR. KALODNER. Lovely, ladies. Just lovely. *(Points at Barry.)* All right, Barry.

(BARRY begins to drag himself up to the front, empty-handed.)

MR. KALODNER. Barry, where is your report?
BARRY. I memorized it, Mr. Kalodner.
MR. KALODNER. Oh, you did?
BARRY. The problem is I have a really bad memory.
MR. KALODNER. The report, Mr. Bockman.

(Defeated, BARRY takes his position. The LIGHTS dim. BARRY starts to sing, but has no idea where it's heading.)

[Music Cue #6: SIR GREENBAUM'S MADRIGAL]

("Greensleeves")

BARRY.
IN SHERWOOD FOREST, THERE DWELT A KNIGHT
WHO WAS KNOWN AS THE RIGHTEOUS SIR ...

(Pause. ALL look at him. HE thinks quickly.)

BARRY.
... GREENBAUM

(HE shrugs, and continues with a little more confidence.)

AND MANY DRAGONS HAD FELT THE MIGHT
OF THE SMITE OF THE RIGHTEOUS SIR GREENBAUM

I CHANCED UPON HIM ONE MORN
WHEN HE'D RECENTLY RESCUED A MAIDEN FAIR
"WHY, WHY ART THOU SO FORLORN?
SIR GREENBAUM, IS THY HEART HEAVY LADEN?"

SAID HE—

(A KNIGHT enters —complete with cardboard armor, a sword that's really a pointer, and a shield with a big "G" on it.)

KNIGHT.
FORSOOTH, 'TIS A SORRY PLIGHT
THAT ENGENDERED MY ATTITUDE BLUEISH
BARRY.
SAID HE—
KNIGHT.
I DON'T WANT TO BE A KNIGHT
THAT'S NO JOB FOR A BOY WHO IS JEWISH

(HE reveals a breastplate decorated with a Star of David.)

BOTH.
ALL DAY WITH THE MIGHTY SWORD
AND THE MIGHTY STEED AND THE MIGHTY LANCE
ALL DAY WITH THAT HEAVY SHIELD
AND A PAIR OF ALUMINUM PANTS

ALL DAY WITH THE SLAYING AND SLEWING
AND SMITING AND SMOTING LIKE ROBIN HOOD
KNIGHT.
OH, WOULDST I COULD KICK THE HABIT
AND GIVE UP SMOTING FOR GOOD
AND SO—
BARRY.
HE SAID TO THE OTHER KNIGHTS—
KNIGHT.
YOU MAY HAVE MY POSSESSIONS AND MY GOODS
FOR I AM MOVING TO SHAKER HEIGHTS
WHERE I'VE GOT SOME CONNECTIONS IN DRY GOODS
BOTH.
FAREWELL TO THE DRAGON'S PAW
AND THE OTHER SWASHBUCKLING GAMES AND SPORTS
KNIGHT.
I'LL WORK FOR MY FATHER-IN-LAW
WHEN I MARRY—
BARRY.
WHEN HE MARRIES—
BOTH.
MISS GUINEVERE SCHWARTZ!

(The TWO pose, then congratulate each other on their impromptu success.)

MR. KALODNER. Thank you, Barry. (*To the "Knight."*) ... And thanks, Morty, glad you could make it.

BARRY. We just wanted to gave you a ... Knight to remember.

(SARAH laughs; MR. K. does not.)

MR. KALODNER. Well, both teams did a fine job. And you've shown that it often takes two individuals working together to accomplish truly historical things. Why, think of Gilbert without Sullivan. Holmes without Watson. Lewis without Clark ... (*Then:)* Or without Dean Martin for that matter. *(Imitates Jerry Lewis:*) "Oh, lady" ... Let's review! (*Each of the KIDS grabs a pointer.*) Class! Everybody's gotta have a "shtick"!

(Each STUDENT uses the pointer as a cane, or a prop, to illustrate a historical tale.)

[Music Cue #7: GOOD ADVICE]

("Good Advice")

MR. KALODNER. (*Sings.*)
SIR ISAAC NEWTON WAS HANGING 'ROUND HIS HOUSE ONE DAY
HIS FACE WAS SUNBURNED AND RED
HE SAID HE DIDN'T WANT TO SLEEP IN THE SHADE OF A TREE
BECAUSE AN APPLE MIGHT FALL ON HIS HEAD

HIS FRIEND SAID "IZZY, DUM-DUM, TAKE MY ADVICE
GO RIGHT BACK THERE AND SLEEP BENEATH THAT TREE
AND IF YOU LET THAT ROTTEN APPLE FALL DOWN ON YOUR HEAD

WHY YOU'LL DISCOVER GRAVITY"

ALL.

AND THAT WAS

MR. KALODNER.

GOOD ADVICE

ALL.

GOOD ADVICE
GOOD ADVICE COSTS NOTHING AND IT'S WORTH THE PRICE
YOU KNOW THE HUMAN RACE IS A MUCH BETTER PLACE
WITH GOOD ADVICE

MR. KALODNER. Sarah!

SARAH. What?

MR. KALODNER. Take it!

SARAH.

WILBUR AND ORVILLE WERE TWO BROTHERS NAMED WRIGHT
THE NICEST PAIR OF KIDS YOU'VE EVER SEEN
THEY WORKED TWELVE YEARS ON A GIFT FOR THEIR MOTHER
THEY THOUGHT IT WAS A WASHING MACHINE

THEIR MOTHER SAID:
"BOYCHICKS, WHAT ARE ALL THOSE WINGS FOR?"
THEY SAID "FOR HANGING CLOTHES OUT TO DRY"
SHE SAID "TAKE THAT WASHING MACHINE OUT TO KITTY HAWK
AND SEE IF THE DARN THING'LL FLY"

ALL.

AND THAT WAS

MR. KALODNER.

GOOD ADVICE

ALL.

GOOD ADVICE
GOOD ADVICE COSTS NOTHING AND IT'S

WORTH THE PRICE
EVERY WORD YOU'RE TOLD COULD BE EIGHTEEN CARAT GOLD
THAT'S GOOD ADVICE

MR. KALODNER. Morty! Louise!

MORTY/LOUISE. Thanks, Mr. K.!

LOUISE. (*Sings.*)

BENJAMIN FRANKLIN WAS A CHARMING OLD MAN
HE WAS ALWAYS FLYING HIS KITE

MORTY.

ONE NIGHT JOHN ADAMS SAID,
"BENJI, WHY AIN'T YOU OUT WITH YOUR KITE?"

LOUISE.

HE SAID, "BECAUSE IT'S RAINING TONIGHT"

MORTY.

JOHN SAID, "BENJI, BUBBY, YOU GO RIGHT BACK OUT THERE
AND TO YOUR KITESTRING TIE A KEY
WELL, THIS MAY SHOCK YOU, BENJI, MY BOY

MORTY/LOUISE.

BUT THAT'S ELECTRICITY"

ALL.

AND THAT WAS

(Singing, as if electrified:)

MR. KALODNER.

GOOD ADVICE

MR. K/BARRY.

GOOD ADVICE

MR. K/BARRY/SARAH.

GOOD ADVICE COSTS NOTHING AND IT'S—

MR. K/BARRY/SARAH/MORTY.

—WORTH THE PRICE

ALL.

IT'S AS HUMBLE AS CAN BE
AND IT'S ABSOLUTELY FREE

THAT'S GOOD ADVICE

(MR. KALODNER taps his pointer on the ground, and organizes a DANCE BREAK.)

MR. KALODNER. (*Speaking in rhythm.*) Alright, class, pop quiz ... Sarah, which anarchists liked spaghetti?

SARAH. It was Sacco and Vanzetti.

MR. KALODNER. Morty, name a Biblical man and his spouse.

MORTY. Must have been Abraham ... and Strauss.

MR. KALODNER. Name the Three Wise Men, Louise.

LOUISE. I don't know, ask Barry, please.

MR. KALODNER. Bockman, now, for extra credit.

BARRY. Curly, Moe and—

MR. KALODNER. Ah, forget it. (*HE leads them in slightly more difficult choreography.*) Alright, class, gets a little harder now.

(The DANCE continues, ending with:)

ALL.
AND THAT WAS GOOD AD … VICE!

(THEY march, revolutionary war style:)

ALL.
GOOD AD ... VICE!

MR. KALODNER. Class Dismissed!

BLACKOUT

[Music Cue #7A: GOOD ADVICE- Playoff]

HE LEAVES HOME

(A loud WHISTLE is heard, cutting off the scene change music.

ESTHER, a loud and over-friendly LADY in a camp sweatshirt, steps into a spotlight. Behind her hangs a sign that reads "Camp Granada.")

ESTHER. *(Enters, blows whistle.)* Hello, hello, boys and girls. I'm Esther Kanner. On behalf of my husband, Arnold Kanner—sit down, darling—I want to welcome the young ladies of Camp Pinecone to the first dance and social gathering of the Summer here at lovely ... Camp Granada! *(Leads applause, which SHE then cuts off with a gesture.)* Camp Granada—the debate champions of the Mohawk Valley ... we may never win a baseball game—but we never lose an argument.

Ladies, there is just one important rule we have tonight—please don't wander away from the festivities here, no matter what anyone tells you. If one of the boys should offer to give you a private tour of our beautiful water ski dock, don't go. We don't have a water ski dock. Get me?!

But don't worry—we've got a lot of fun planned for you. There will be bingo in the Sophie Epstein Rec Hall, punch at the Morris Katz Totem Pole, and a terrific campfire on the Phil Levy God Rest His Soul Baseball Diamond ...

And, boys, remember—there are ladies present, so no putting out the fire the way you did last summer. *(Clears throat.)* Now ... on with the dance!

(SHE blows her whistle and exits.
LIGHTS up.

[Music Cue #7B: CHA-CHA]

MUSIC plays cha-cha underscore of "Hello Muddah." A punchbowl sits on a table. There are streamers across the inside of a recreation hall.

BARRY, now 13, dances on awkwardly with his nerdy, but optimistic, friend, LEONARD. BOTH hold glasses of punch.)

LEONARD. 1, 2, cha-cha-cha ... 3, 4, cha-cha-cha...

(The dance practice is not going well.)

BARRY. 1, 2 ... 1, 2 ... What am I doing wrong, Leonard?

LEONARD. I think you're missing a cha.

BARRY. Oh, never mind.

(THEY stop dancing and drink from their punch glasses. THEY look out front.)

BARRY. Gee, there they are ...

(THEY nervously look across the imaginary dance floor at the girls of Camp Pinecone.)

LEONARD. What a sight. The forty-five most luscious adolescent goddesses in the Lake Wanatootsie region. It's like the World Series of Puberty.

BARRY. Wow ...

LEONARD. That's about two million dollars of orthodontia out there.

BARRY. Maybe I could tell them one of my jokes ...

LEONARD. No, don't make them smile. You could be blinded. (*Pulls out a telescope and focuses out front.*) I've been tracking this cute one with curly hair all night. (*Pointing to women.*) Who do you like?

BARRY. (*Looks in the distance.*) Oh, I don't know. How 'bout the blonde with the long legs?

LEONARD. (*Still looking through telescope.*) He's the bus driver. *(Panic stricken.)* Oh, where did she go? I lost her. (*Starts off.*)

BARRY. Hey, don't leave me here. Leonard!...

LEONARD. (*Exiting.*) Ask somebody to dance!

BARRY. (*Calling after.*) I will ... in a little while ... I'm just waiting for my voice to change ... (*BARRY attempts a few steps unsuccessfully.*)

[Music Cue #8: I CAN'T DANCE]

(Grieg: "Norwegian Dance #2")

BARRY. (*Sings.*)
I CAN'T DANCE
I CAN'T DANCE
BESIDES I'M TWO FEET SHORTER THAN THE GIRLS ARE
ALL THESE STUPID DANCES ARE JUST PLAIN DUMB
WHEN THEY ASKED I SHOULD'VE SAID I CAN'T COME
THERE'S A GIRL WITH BRACES
STANDING BY THE PUNCHBOWL
AND SHE'S MAKING FUNNY FACES
I GUESS SHE WANTS TO DANCE

(CARLOTTA enters across the stage, a freckle-faced girl with glasses, and another wallflower. SHE carries a punch glass.)

CARLOTTA.
I CAN'T DANCE
I CAN'T DANCE
BESIDES I LOOK SO AWFUL IN THESE BRACES
IF THAT BOY WANTS ME TO DANCE I'LL JUST DIE
I'M SO TALL AND HE'S ABOUT THREE FEET

HIGH
EVER SINCE SEPTEMBER, I'VE BEEN TAKING DANCING LESSONS
NOW I CAN'T REMEMBER HOW THE HECK TO DANCE

(BARRY approaches her awkwardly.)

BARRY.
PARDON ME, I'M BARRY
AND I DON'T MIND IF YOU ARE TALL AND SKINNY
AND THOSE BRACES ON YOUR TEETH—THEY'RE REAL NEAT

CARLOTTA.
THANK YOU FOR THE COMPLIMENT
GEE, YOU'RE SWEET

BARRY.
YOUR NAME IS CARLOTTA
I MET YOU LAST SUMMER WHEN YOU CAME TO CAMP GRANADA
YOU WANNA TRY TO DANCE?

(BARRY takes her punch glass, crushes it gallantly, then disposes of it awkwardly. THEY struggle to get into dancing position, then collide.)

BARRY.
RIGHT FOOT FIRST, LEFT FOOT NEXT
I THINK YOU'RE S'POSED TO DO IT TO THE MUSIC

CARLOTTA.
YOU DON'T REALLY LOOK SO BAD
JUST YOUR EARS

BARRY.
WHEN D'YA TAKE YOUR BRACES OFF?

CARLOTTA.
FOUR MORE YEARS

BARRY.
BY THE TIME YOUR TEETH ARE READY
I'LL BE TWO FEET TALLER
AND I'LL ASK YOU TO GO STEADY
TOGETHER.
THEN ... WE'LL ... DANCE!

(THEY shake hands awkwardly.)

CARLOTTA. So, Barry, what are you doing this summer?

BARRY. I spend most of my time at the nature shack. I feed the mice and gerbils ...

CARLOTTA. How sweet.

BARRY. ... to the snakes. How do you like Camp Pinecone?

CARLOTTA. It's okay, I guess. I'm in the drama club.

BARRY. An actress?! Wow!

CARLOTTA. Yeah, it's fun even though it's all girls. So far, we did "The Queen and I" ... "Twelve Angry Women" ... and "Dolls and Dolls."

(A dramatic CHORD.

[Music Cue #9: KISS OF MYER]

MYER, a very cool 14-year-old comes onstage, combing his hair dramatically to musical flourishes. HE looks at Carlotta. SHE swoons, and completely forgets about Barry.)

BARRY. Hey, Myer! I was just gonna make my move.

MYER. Yeah, right. The summer only has eight weeks. Go away, Barney. (*Kisses Carlotta.*)

BARRY. That's Barry. Come on, Carlotta.

CARLOTTA. *(Lips pressed against MYER's.)* Go away, Barney.

(BARRY trudges off. SARAH runs on from the other side of the stage, now also 13 years old.)

SARAH. (*Calling behind her.*) Leonard, that better be a telescope in your pocket, or I'm telling!...

(All of a sudden, SARAH sees Myer, and is stricken. MYER kisses SARAH.)

SARAH. Who is that?
CARLOTTA. Myer Myer Pants on Fire ...
MYER. (*Swinging his hips.*)
DIGHTY DIGHTY DIGHTY DIGH ...

(The GIRLS swing back, and echo.)

GIRLS.
DIGHTY DIGHTY DIGHTY DIGH ...
MYER.
DIGHTY DIGHTY DIGHTY DIGH ...
GIRLS.
DIGHTY DIGHTY DIGHTY DIGH ...

(MYER unleashes an ultra-sexy and dramatic DIGHTY DIGHTY DIGH, then dares the girls to match it. THEY can only growl.)

GIRLS. Grrrrr ...

("Kiss of Fire")

MYER.
THE GIRLS GO CRAZY WHEN THEY GET A KISS FROM MYER
THE KISS OF MYER IS THE ACME OF DESIRE
THE KISS OF MYER MAKES THEIR TEMPERATURE GET HIGHER
THE KISS OF MYER LIT THE GREAT CHICAGO FIRE
GIRLS.
HE HAS A WAY THAT MAKES THE LADIES FEEL

EXALTED
HE'LL TAKE YOU OUT AND TREAT YOU TO A CHOCOLATE MALTED
THEN SOME PISTACHIO NUTS

MYER.
A NICKEL'S WORTH

GIRLS.
UNSALTED

MYER.
AND AFTER THAT, LITTLE GIRL, YOU'RE THROUGH

GIRLS.
HE'LL TRY TO LURE YOU, ONE NIGHT WHEN STARS ARE TWINKLY
HE'LL CALL AND SAY:

MYER.
COME OVER, WE'LL WATCH TV, MY PET

GIRLS. (*Sigh, then:*)
BUT I ASSURE YOU, YOU'LL SEE NO DAVID BRINKLEY

MYER.
'CAUSE MYER HASN'T GOT A TV SET

SARAH.
WHAT DOES HE NEED IT?

CARLOTTA.
HE'D NEVER USE IT

GIRLS.
TO HIM "THE LATE LATE SHOW" IS YOU!

MYER.
THE KISS OF MYER IS SO SWEET THAT NONE IS SWEETER
THE GIRLS CAN'T WAIT FOR ME TO COME AND READ THEIR METER
I'M KNOWN ALL OVER AS "THE BRONX LA DOLCE VITA"

GIRLS.
THE CARY GRANT OF THE GRAND CONCOURSE
WHATEVER MYER WANTS ... MYER GETS

MYER.
AND THAT'S MY NAME ...
MY NAME IS MYER GETZ!
GIRLS.
HIS NAME IS MYER GETZ!

(The THREE end in a passionate embrace.)

MYER. (*To Carlotta.*) Come on, sweetheart. Let's go somewhere and you can show me your ... lanyards.

CARLOTTA. I think I'd rather see the water ski dock ...

MYER. *(Impressed.)* O-kay!

(THEY exit.)

SARAH. (*Running after Myer and Carlotta.*) Hey, I have nice lanyards ... (*SHE exits.*)

(The SOUND of thunder and lightning, and BARRY is revealed—despondent, holding a pencil and paper. HE composes a letter.)

[Music Cue #10: HELLO MUDDAH,
HELLO FADDUH!]

("Dance of the Hours")

BARRY.
HELLO, MUDDAH - HELLO, FADDUH
HERE I AM AT CAMP GRANADA
CAMP IS VERY ENTERTAINING
AND THEY SAY WE'LL HAVE SOME FUN IF IT STOPS RAINING

I WENT HIKING WITH JOE SPIVEY
HE DEVELOPED POISON IVY
YOU REMEMBER LEONARD SKINNER

HE GOT PTOMAINE POISONING LAST NIGHT AFTER DINNER

ALL THE COUNSELORS HATE THE WAITERS
AND THE LAKE HAS ALLIGATORS
AND THE HEAD COACH WANTS NO SISSIES
SO HE READS TO US FROM SOMETHING CALLED "ULYSSES"

NOW I DON'T WANT THIS SHOULD SCARE YA
BUT MY BUNKMATE HAS MALARIA
YOU REMEMBER JEFFREY HARDY?
THEY'RE ABOUT TO ORGANIZE A SEARCHING PARTY

TAKE ME HOME, OH MUDDAH, FADDUH
TAKE ME HOME, I HATE GRANADA
DON'T LEAVE ME OUT IN THE FOREST WHERE
I MIGHT GET EATEN BY A BEAR

TAKE ME HOME, I PROMISE I WILL NOT MAKE NOISE
OR MESS THE HOUSE WITH OTHER BOYS
OH, PLEASE DON'T MAKE ME STAY
I'VE BEEN HERE ONE WHOLE DAY ...

(The MUSIC continues. We see SARAH, alone and crying, as SHE comes back into the hall.)

BARRY. Sarah Jackman?

SARAH. Barry Bockman?

BARRY. What are you doing here? I thought you went to the Catskills this summer.

SARAH. Shecky Green insulted my mother at Grossinger's so we left. I'm miserable.

BARRY. I'm miserable, too.

SARAH. Really? (*Gets an idea.*) Hey, maybe we could be miserable ... together?

BARRY. That would be *fun*!

SARAH. Okay. I'll be right back: I just want to get a tissue.

BARRY. (*That kidder.*) Tissue!? I hardly know you!!!

(THEY do their special goofy laugh.)

SARAH. Oh, Barry, you're so funny ...

(SHE runs out happily. BARRY smiles after her, then turns with renewed energy.)

BARRY.
WAIT A MINUTE, IT STOPPED HAILING
GUYS ARE SWIMMING, GUYS ARE SAILING
PLAYING BASEBALL, GEE, THAT'S BETTER
MUDDAH, FADDUH, KINDLY DISREGARD THIS LETTER!

(HE signs the letter.)

BLACKOUT

[Music Cue #10A: Scene Change 2]

HE GROWS UP

[Music Cue #10B: POMP AND CIRCUMSTANCE]

(In the BLACKOUT, we hear "Pomp and Circumstance." Over the MUSIC, a typical High School PRINCIPAL enters, and addresses the audience:)

PRINCIPAL. Students, Parents, Teachers, and Friends—as Principal of Herbert Hoover High School, I want to welcome you to this year's Commencement Exercises. Thank you, thank you ... I looked up the word "commencement" in the dictionary last night, and it said: "A large Australian rodent." (*Chuckles.*) No ... I'm teasing ... it's a "*beginning*"!... heh heh. And to *begin* this morning, please welcome the Herbert Hoover High School Senior Chorus. (*To an audience member, as the CHOIR enters:*) I thought the rodent joke would get a bigger laugh ...

(LIGHTS up on the CHOIR as PRINCIPAL joins them—all present but BARRY—in robes, holding music folders. ALL sing a capella:)

[Music Cue #11: NO ONE'S PERFECT]

("Cornell Alma Mater")

CHORUS.
WHEN THE HOOVER HIGH SCHOOL CHORUS
SINGS A SONG LIKE THIS
BARRY. (*Running on, late.*)
LIKE THIS, LIKE THIS, LIKE THIS

(Sings sotto, to the others.)

(SORRY...)
CHORUS.
EVERY SINGLE NOTE IS GORGEOUS
BUT WE SOMETIMES MISS

(THEY hit an off-key note.)

NO ONE'S PERFECT, NO ONE'S PERFECT
NO ONE'S PERFECT, PAL

THAT INCLUDES:

FRED WARING AND HIS PENNSYLVANIANS
AND THE NEW CHRISTY MINSTRELS
(WHO WERE MADE FAMOUS BY THEIR FREQUENT APPEARANCES ON THE TONIGHT SHOW)
AND THE MORMON TABERNACLE CHOIR
AND THE ROBERT SHAW CHORALE

(One of the girls continues in an off-key SOPRANO.)

CHORUS.
FAR ABOVE THE OTHER SINGERS IN THE TREBLE CLEF
A SOPRANO SINGS IN B-FLAT, BUT THE KEY IS "F"

(The SOPRANO, oblivious, smiles.)

NO ONE'S PERFECT, NO ONE'S PERFECT
WE HAVE LEARNED TONIGHT
SO YOU'LL BE ASTOUNDED WHEN WE HIT THIS LAST NOTE ...

(THEY proceed gingerly.)

... RIGHT

(It is a half-step flat, but the piano bangs out the right note, and THEY bring it up to pitch. The CHORUS smiles and bows.

[Music Cue #11A: Scene Change 3]

ALL but SARAH and BARRY exit. THEY both remove their robes to reveal college clothing. BARRY wears the letters of the Zeta Beta Tau fraternity.

A SIGN: BRONX ZOO. The SOUND of animal noises. BARRY, carrying a bookbag, walks with SARAH, who is carrying a textbook and a notebook.)

SARAH. What a great idea to study at the Bronx Zoo, Barry.

BARRY. Well, it was so noisy back at the frat house. Besides, they say it's always better when you study with a close close friend. (*Starts to get carried away.*) Two young people studying together ... side by side ... page by page ... word by word ... their hot breath warming the cold hard ...

(SARAH looks at him blankly.)

BARRY. (*Changing tactics.*) Look, there's the hippopotamuses!

SARAH. That would be Hippopotam-*i*. Listen, why don't I give you some review questions?

BARRY. Okay. Fine.

SARAH. Now the first question has to do with—

(As THEY find seats, BARRY suavely offers food from his bookbag.)

BARRY. Mint?

SARAH. No, thanks. The first question—

BARRY. (*Pulling out a bottle of Manischewitz.*) Wine?

SARAH. No. Thanks. Question One: In what geographical region are you most likely to find the giraffe?

BARRY. Great Neck.

(SARAH shoots him a look.)

BARRY. It was a guess.

SARAH. Question Two: Name a land animal, found in Mexico, known for its great agility.

BARRY. Cheetah.

SARAH. Found in Mexico.

BARRY. Cheetah ... Rivera.

SARAH. (*Closes the book.*) Barry, if you're not gonna be serious, I'm going to catch the next bus back.

BARRY. I'm sorry, Sarah. I'm just trying to make the date more enjoyable.

SARAH. The what?

BARRY. (*Into his hand, muffled.*) The date.

SARAH. Barry, this isn't a date. It's homework. (*Starts a nervous giggle.*) A date ... how silly. I've known you since I was born. (*More laughter.*)

BARRY. (*Embarrassed.*) Yeah, I was just kidding, Sarah ... ha ha ...

SARAH. Um ... Question Three: What living creature can carry two hundred times its own date? (*Realizes.*) —*weight*! I mean *weight*!

BARRY. (*Jumping up.*) You said date.

SARAH. I didn't!

BARRY. You did!

SARAH. You just have me so mixed up! (*Starts to exit.*) I'm leaving. I have to catch the next boyfriend back. (*Realizes.*) Oh, darn.

BARRY. (*Moving toward her.*) Sarah—

SARAH. Stay back. Just talk to the camels and the giraffes and the hippopotamuses?

BARRY. Hippopotami.

SARAH. (*Giving up.*) Oh, who cares?

BARRY. *They* do. One hippopotamus is lonely. One hippopotami is never alone.

[Music Cue #12: ONE HIPPOPOTAMI]

(*"One Hippopotami"*)

(*MUSIC creeps in.*)

BARRY. (*Sings.*)
ONE HIPPOPOTAMI CANNOT GET ON A BUS
BECAUSE ONE HIPPOPOTAMI IS TWO HIPPOPOTAMUS

SARAH. (*Nervously.*) That's very interesting, Barry ... I didn't know that ...

BARRY.
AND IF YOU HAVE TWO GOOSE
THAT MAKES ONE GEESE
A PAIR OF MOUSE IS MICE
A PAIR OF MOOSE

SARAH.
IS MEESE

(Realizes.)

... MOOSES .... MOOSE ...

BARRY.
A PARANOIA IS A BUNCH OF MENTAL BLOCKS
AND WHEN JOYCE BROTHERS MEETS KILDARE
THAT'S CALLED A ...

(SHE gets it, and joins:)

BOTH.
PAIR-O'-DOCS

(THEY laugh. BARRY moves in closer.)

BARRY.
WHEN TWO MINKS FALL IN LOVE
WITH ALL THEIR HEART AND SOUL
YOU'LL FIND THE PLURAL OF TWO MINKS IS ONE MINK STOLE

(SARAH moves away, but not too far.)

SARAH. (*Changing the subject.*)
SINGULARS AND PLURALS ARE SO DIFFERENT BLESS MY SOUL

BARRY.
HAS IT EVER OCCURRED TO YOU

THAT THE PLURAL OF HALF IS WHOLE?

SARAH.
A BUNCH OF TOOTH IS TEETH
A GROUP OF FOOT IS FEET

BARRY.
AND TWO CANARIES MAKE A PAIR
THEY CALL IT

BOTH.
A PAIR-A-KEET

SARAH.
A PARAMECIUM IS NOT A PAIR
A PARALLELOGRAM—

BARRY.
—IS JUST A CRAZY SQUARE

SARAH.
NOBODY KNOWS JUST WHAT A PARAPHERNALIA IS
AND WHAT IS HALF A PAIR OF SCISSORS?

BARRY.
IT'S A SINGLE "SCIS"

(HE moves closer again, this time SARAH stays.)

BOTH.
WITH SOMEONE YOU ADORE
IF YOU SHOULD FIND ROMANCE

BARRY.
YOU'LL PANT AND PANT ONCE MORE

BOTH.
AND THAT'S A PAIR OF PANTS!

(THEY kiss tentatively, pull back, then embrace passionately, as the LIGHTS fade out.)

HE IS WED

(On tape, a voice says: "Sarah and Barry, I now pronounce you Man and Wife. Barry, you may step on

the glass for good luck." There is the sound of a stomp. A pause. "Try it again, Barry" ... Then we hear the glass being smashed, followed by a loud "Ouch" from Barry.

[Music Cue #12A: SAMBA]

LIGHTS come up. As the now visible BAND finishes a samba version of "Hello, Muddah"—a late MIDDLE-AGED COUPLE dances by an enormous wedding cake, and poses.)

HARVEY. How ' bout a hand for that band?! What a band!? "Noah and the Noodniks." They're great!

SHEILA. And expensive, Harvey!

HARVEY. And expensive. That's right, Sheila. (*Still smiling, but annoyed.*) You want me to tell everyone what they get?

SHEILA. Five thousand dollars.

HARVEY. Five thou—Hey! It doesn't matter. (*Pause.*) Fifty-two hundred. Now! As father of the bride, I want to tell you that my lovely Sarah, and her new husband ... (*SHEILA cues him subtly; HE barely flinches.*) *Barry*—will be back from the emergency room shortly. And I want to welcome you on behalf of my wife and our two other daughters Beatrice and Kaye—

SHEILA.—who married a dentist and a dermatologist respectively.

(BAND: drumroll.)

[Music Cue #12B: BUFFET FANFARE]

HARVEY. Ah, at last! The moment we've all been waiting for—(*Silence.*)—The buffet is now open! (*Fanfare.*) And what a gorgeous spread.

SHEILA. Beautiful spread.

HARVEY. It really is lovely. Did you all see that amazing, completely edible sculpture of Abba Eban?

SHEILA. He's Israeli.

HARVEY. That's right, Sheil.
SHEILA. From Israel.
HARVEY. Right, Sheil. A completely edible Abba Eban! And that ain't chopped liver.

(A VOICE from off-stage:)

VOICE. You're right! It's tuna salad!

(The black sheep of the family, PHIL, suddenly appears and joins Harvey and Sheila.)

PHIL. Hello, everybody!

(Fanfare.)

HARVEY. Oh, no. It's your brother.
PHIL. Sheil, how's my *older* sister?
SHEILA. (*Trying to whisper.*) Phil, what are you doing?
PHIL. What? I can't come up and toast my beautiful niece. Where's my little kneidle anyway?
HARVEY. (*To Sheila.*) We only picked this date 'cause he said he couldn't make it.
PHIL. Oh, I'm sorry—I can't stand with the great Harvey Jackman. Pardon me, Mr. Big Shot Accountant. *(PHIL mimes kissing Harvey's ring.)*
SHEILA. Phil!
PHIL. Come on! It's a wedding! Let's all sing! I'll go first. (*PHIL hands a very long musical arrangement to the BAND LEADER.*)
HARVEY. (*To Sheila.*) I told you this would happen!
PHIL. (*Sings.*) "I told you this would happen ..."
SHEILA. All right, Harv, let him sing. Maybe then he'll sit down.

(HARVEY glares at Phil as HE and SHEILA exit.)

HARVEY. Phil, you're out of the will.

PHIL. (*Sings.*) "Phil you're out the will." Hey, that rhymes, Harvey. Good! Take it away, Noodniks! (*Grabs a microphone:*) Good evening, ladies and gentlemen. It's great to be here. Harvey and Sheila, this one's for you. (*Sings.*)

[Music Cue #13: PHIL MEDLEY]

(Auth. Note: PHIL should physically interact with audience as much as possible.)

HELLO MUDDAH, HELLO FADDUH
HERE WE ARE AT TEMPLE MASADA
WHAT A LOVELY, LOVELY CHUPAH
AND THAT WAITRESS LOOKS SO GOOD THAT I COULD SHTUPA ...

(HARVEY marches back out, but SHEILA catches him by the arm and pulls him off.)

PHIL. Thank you. It's great to be here. With all my friends and ... some of my family. There's my neighbors, Al and Yetta Cohen. (*Sings.)*

("Alouette")

AL AND YETTA—ALWAYS SIT TO-GETTA
WATCHING TV EV'RY SINGLE NIGHT

(*Speaks.)* Thank you. And now a special Philharmonic tribute to my great Uncle Seymour sitting right here—92 years young today, ladies and gentlemen. I love that man! (*To Seymour's "neighbor.*") Wipe his chin, will ya? (*Sings.*)

("Auld Lang Syne")

I KNOW A MAN NAMED SEYMOUR LANG AND HE HAS A NEON SIGN
AND SEYMOUR LANG IS VERY OLD
SO THEY CALL IT "OLD LANG'S SIGN"

(*Speaks.*) Thank you. I see my cousin Lou made it in from the Island. How you doing, Mr. H!? (*Sings.*)

("Harrigan")

H-O-R-O-W-I-T-Z SPELLS BIGAMIST

(*Speaks.*) Thank you. Sorry, Mrs. H … Noah, I'd like to bring it down a little bit. (*Loosens his tie.*) I want to dedicate this to my beautiful, new, 22-year-old (ouch) wife ... Vicki. (*Blows a kiss out to "Vicki."*) Darling, this one's ... pour vous ... (*Sings.*)

WHEN I'M IN THE MOOD FOR LOVE
YOU'RE IN THE MOOD FOR HERRING ....

Thank you.

(Now HARVEY marches on, SHEILA behind.)

PHIL. Oh, well, I see that my time is up.
HARVEY. Goodbye, Phil.
PHIL. I'm leaving. I'm leaving. (*Returns for a finale.*) But ... before I go, I want everybody here to join me over at Harvey and Sheila's house later. You remember how to get there, don't you? Noah! (*Sings, while avoiding Harvey.*)
HARVEY. He's singing again!

("Give My Regards to Broadway")

PHIL.
GET ON THE GARDEN FREEWAY

WHEN YOU COME OUT TO VISIT ME
YOU'LL SEE A GREAT BIG SHOPPING CENTER
WITH A BRAND NEW A&P

Sheil, you'll love it!

SHEILA. I've been there!

PHIL.

TURN LEFT AT HOWARD JOHNSON'S
CONTINUE TO THE THIRD STOP LIGHT
THEN TURN AROUND AND DRIVE RIGHT BACK
BECAUSE I WON'T BE THERE
(AND I DON'T REALLY CARE)
I WON'T BE THERE TONIGHT!

(*PHIL waves and exits.*) Thank you! I love you all!

[Music Cue #13A: PHIL - Playoff]

HARVEY. (*Furiously cutting off the band; then:*) Woo. That was fun. Thank you, Phil, and thank you, Noah and the fifty-two-hundred-dollar Noodniks.

[Music Cue #13B: WEDDING MARCH]

(HARVEY is interrupted by the band playing the "WEDDING MARCH" as SARAH and a limping BARRY enter.)

HARVEY. Finally, our happy couple is back!

BARRY. (*Sheepishly looks at his bandaged foot, then turns to the Guests.)* You should see the glass.

(HARVEY kisses SARAH, SHEILA kisses BARRY, making "muh" sound. HARVEY goes to kiss BARRY, thinks better of it, and just grabs his face.)

SHEILA. Barry, say a few words.

BARRY. Ladies and gentlemen—

HARVEY. (*Moving BARRY aside.*) Great speech.

Now—it's my turn. [*Music Cue #14: HARVEY AND SHEILA]* I've worked up a little presentation with the band. A little tribute to my pride, my joy, my eternal darling, Sheila Jackman.

(The BAND begins to play.)

SHEILA. What a surprise?! I had no idea. (*To Band.*) In E flat!

(BAND modulates.)

HARVEY. After all, next Thursday is our twenty-seventh wedding anniversary.
SHEILA. He remembered!
HARVEY. And I just want to say:

("Hava Nagila")

HARVEY AND SHEILA
HARVEY AND SHEILA
HARVEY AND SHEILA
HARVEY/SHEILA.
OH, THE DAY WE MET!
SHEILA.
HARVEY
HARVEY.
AND SHEILA
SHEILA.
HARVEY
HARVEY.
AND SHEILA
SHEILA.
HARVEY (*Nudges HARVEY, who is waving into the audience.*)
HARVEY.
...SHEILA

BOTH.
NO ONE WILL FORGET
SHEILA.
HARVEY'S A—
HARVEY.
C.P.A.
SHEILA.
HE WORKS FOR—
HARVEY.
I.B.M.
SHEILA.
HE WENT TO—
HARVEY.
M.I.T.
SHEILA.
AND GOT HIS—
HARVEY.
PH.D.
SHEILA'S A GIRL I KNOW
SHEILA.
AT BBD&O
HARVEY.
SHE WORKS—
SHEILA.
THE PBX
HARVEY.
AND MAKES OUT THE CHECKS
ALL.
THEN CAME ONE GREAT DAY WHEN
BARRY/SARAH.
HARVEY TOOK THE ELEVATOR
SHEILA GOT IN TWO FLOORS LATER
SOON THEY FELT THAT THEY WERE FALLING
EVERYONE HEARD SHEILA CALLING
SHEILA.
"RING THE BELL!"
HARVEY. (*Struck by love.*)
BUT WE FELL

ALL.
HARV AND SHEILA FELL IN LOVE

(Tempo picks up.)

SHEILA. Chupah!
ALL.
HARVEY AND SHEILA
HARVEY AND SHEILA
HARVEY AND SHEILA
SHEILA.
CHOSE A WEDDING RING

(As OTHERS sing, showing off her ring.)

What a rock, hunh?... 5200 Dollars ... Bought it from Cousin Sid ... Wholesale ...
ALL.
HARVEY AND SHEILA
HARVEY AND SHEILA
HARVEY AND SHEILA
HARVEY.
MARRIED IN THE SPRING
SARAH.
SHE SHOPPED AT A & P
BARRY.
HE BOUGHT A USED MG
SHEILA.
HE SAT AND WATCHED TV
HARVEY.
ON THE RCA
SARAH.
BORROWED
HARVEY.
FROM HFC
BARRY.
BOUGHT SOME—

SHEILA.
AT&T
ALL.
AND ON ELECTION DAY, WORKED FOR JFK
THEN THEY WENT AND GOT A
CREDIT CARD FROM R.H. MACY
BOUGHT A LAYETTE, PINK AND LACY
THEN THEY HAD TWIN BABY GIRLS
BOTH WITH DIMPLES, BOTH WITH CURLS
ONE NAMED BEA
SHEILA. (*Reminding.*) Dentist!
ALL.
ONE NAMED KAYE
SHEILA. Dermatologist!
ALL. (*Dovening.)*
SOON THEY JOINED THE P.T.A...

(PHIL enters, and joins in.)

ALL.
HARVEY AND SHEILA
PHIL. Thank you!
ALL.
HARVEY AND SHEILA
HARVEY AND SHEILA
MOVED TO WEST L.A.

HARVEY AND SHEILA
HARVEY AND SHEILA
HARVEY AND SHEILA
FLEW T.W.A.

(HARVEY grabs for Phil but it turns into a bunny hop.)

ALL.
THEY BOUGHT A HOUSE ONE DAY
FINANCED BY F.H.A.
IT HAD A SWIMMING POOL—FULL OF H_20

TRADED THEIR USED MG FOR A NEW XKE
SWITCHED TO THE G.O.P.
THAT'S THE WAY THINGS GO

OH, THAT HARVEY, HE WAS REALLY SMART
HE USED HIS NOODLE
SHEILA BOUGHT A WHITE FRENCH POODLE
WENT TO EUROPE WITH HER VISA
HARVEY'S RICH, THEY SAY THAT HE'S A
V.I.P.
THIS COULD BE ...
ONLY IN THE U.S.A!

(STAGING IF POSSIBLE: During the above paragraph, PHIL pulls someone out of the audience to get between himself and HARVEY.
While ALL sing "U.S.A.," THEY salute, then indicate that the audience member should salute as well.)

HARVEY. (*To new "guest."*) So, did you bring a gift?

SHEILA. (*Nervously.*) Dance!

(A wild DANCE follows, in which HARVEY and PHIL Kazatzky, and the MEMBER OF THE AUDIENCE ends up in the middle of a HORA. After the dance:)

HARVEY. (*Who has gotten the name during the dance.*) Let's have a big hand for Cousin (Ellen)!

(THEY help the audience member back to his/her seat.)

HARVEY. Phil, make yourself useful, turn up the lights! (*To Barry.*) Give me the microphone ... uh ...

BARRY. (*Into mike.*) Barry.

HARVEY. ... Barry. All right, folks, now it's time for some responsive singing.

(The HOUSELIGHTS come up and HARVEY divides the "guests"—the audience—into three sections. HE teaches each section a vocal part in turn:)

HARVEY. (*House left.*) Let's begin with the Groom's side first ... which is all you people over here, etc. (*Teaches them their part; BOOM BOOM BOOM etc.*) Come on, Mr. Bockman, you're not paying for this, at least sing ... (*Then, after:*) What do you expect from the Groom's side? Now, my lovely Bride's side ... which is everyone over here, etc. (*House right. Teaches them their part: HARVEY AND SHEILA, ETC. OH THE DAY THEY MET.*) Grandma, take the silverware out of your purse. Now. Gentiles in the back! Gentiles, when I point to you, I want *you* all to sing ... "We Wish You A Merry Christmas, We Wish you ..." Heh heh ... No, I kid you, Gentiles. What you're going to sing is: (*Teaches them: DAI DAI DAI etc. NOTE: If a few sing, "Good. Both of you." If several sing, "I didn't know we invited so many, Sheil ..."*) Okay, now let's put it all together, one group at a time! Here we go! (*Finally, after singing-along twice through, HARVEY yells:*) Now In Hebrew!

(ALL are silent, then laugh.)

HARVEY. I want to make a toast! Quickly, come on! Come together, everyone! The band is on overtime, come. (*Raises his glass.*) To my lovely daughter, Sarah, and her new husband ...

SHEILA. Barry.

HARVEY. (*Without blinking an eye.*) Barry ... May you two be as happy with each other as—Sheila is with me.

(SHEILA knows something is wrong with the toast, but isn't exactly sure what...)

HARVEY. Noah! (*Sings.*)
YOU'RE IN LOVE
PHIL.
GOD'S ABOVE
BARRY. It's a great party, Mrs. Jackman.
SHEILA. Call me Mom.
BARRY. Thanks, Mom. (*To Harvey.*) Thanks, Dad.
HARVEY. Call me Mr. Jackman.
ALL. (*Sing.*)
AND WE WISH YOU MAZEL TOV! HEY!

BLACKOUT

END OF ACT I

(*A slide comes up:*)

HE INTERMISHES

ACT II

[Music Cue #15:ENTR'ACTE]

HE REPRODUCES

(The BAND plays an ENTR'ACTE, as the lights go out. In the DARK, the sound of a BABY's cry, followed by LIGHTS up on BARRY and SARAH, wearing hospital gowns, standing behind their new baby, ROBBIE, in his carriage. HARVEY and SHEILA, the proud grandparents, stand nearby.)

[Music Cue #16: ROBBIE]

("Mary's a Grand Old Name")

ALL.
WE'LL CALL HIM ROBBIE, ROBBIE
THAT'LL BE THE BABY'S NAME ...

ROBBIE. Hello, Muddah! Hello, Fadduh! (*Sees Grandparents.*) Harvey, Sheila!

(The DOORBELL rings. MUSIC.)

BARRY. Come on in! Coats on the left! Gifts on the right! Meet Robbie Bockman, My Son ... The Infant!

[Music Cue #17: SHAKE HANDS WITH YOUR UNCLE MAX]

("Shake Hands With Your Uncle Mike")

BARRY.
SHAKE HANDS WITH YOUR UNCLE MAX, MY BOY

SARAH.
AND HERE IS HIS SISTER SHIRL
SHEILA.
AND HERE IS YOUR COUSIN ISABEL
HARVEY.
THAT'S IRVING'S OLDEST GIRL
SARAH.
AND YOU REMEMBER THE TISHMAN TWINS
GERALD AND JEROME
ALL.
THEY ALL CAME OUT TO GREET YOU
AND TO WISH YOU WELCOME HOME

MEET—
MAROWITZ, BAROWITZ, HANDELMAN, SHANDLEMAN
SPERBER AND GERBER AND STEINER AND STONE
MOSCOWITZ, LUPOWITZ, ARONSON, BERENSON
KLEINMAN AND FEINMAN AND FRIEDMAN AND COHEN
HARVEY.
SMALLOWITZ
SARAH.
WALLOWITZ
SHEILA.
TEITLEBAUM
BARRY.
MANDLEBAUM
SHEILA.
LEVIN
SARAH.
LEVINSKY
BARRY.
LEVINE
HARVEY.
AND LEVI

SHEILA.
BRUMBERGER
SARAH.
SCHLUMBERGER
HARVEY.
MINCUS
BARRY.
AND PINCUS
HARVEY/SHEILA.
STEIN WITH AN "E-I"
BARRY/SARAH.
AND STYNE WITH A "Y"

(The bassinet is wheeled around happily.)

BARRY.
SHAKE HANDS WITH YOUR UNCLE SOL, MINE BOY
SARAH.
AND HERE IS YOUR UNCLE SID
SHEILA.
AND HERE IS YOUR COUSIN YETTA
HARVEY.
WHO EXPECTS ANOTHER KID
MEN.
WHENEVER YOU'RE ON THE ROAD, MY BOY
WOMEN.
WHEREVER YOU MAY ROAM
ALL.
WE'LL ALL BE HERE WHEN YOU COME BACK
TO WISH YOU WELCOME HOME !

(The BABY joins in the chord.)

HARVEY. He harmonizes! (*Walking BARRY to the side.*) Now listen ...
ALL. Barry.
HARVEY. Barry ... I think we should have a talk.

BARRY. Sure, Mr. Jackman.

HARVEY. Call me Grandpa.

BARRY. (*Putting arm around Harvey.*) Okay, Grandpa.

HARVEY. (*On second thought:*) Call me Mr. Jackman. You and Sarah have been living here with us since the day you got married, and honestly, it's been a great three years ... four months, twelve days, six hours —(*Checks watch.*) and eighteen minutes. But now with the baby and everything, I think it's time you considered getting a place of your own.

SHEILA. Harvey, you're not gonna take that little poodlecake away from me, are you? Are you? Are you? (*Breaks into tears.*)

HARVEY. She'll get over it. (*Unfolds a pile of graph paper.*) Now I've taken all the towns in Westchester, New Jersey, and both shores of Long Island, and rated them on a scale of one to ten with regard to school system, commuting distance, country club membership—

SHEILA. *(Still bereft.*) Are you?

HARVEY. —and proximity to Grandma. I ran some numbers with the boys at the office, and let me lay out all your options: You're moving to New Rochelle.

BARRY. Um ... we need a little time to find a house.

SHEILA. It's gorgeous. Four bedrooms, eat-in kitchen, covered patio, finished basement.

HARVEY. (*Flipping over the keys.*) You'll love it.

SARAH. Daddy, we do need a little time to think about it.

HARVEY. No problem! The movers won't be here till six.

(SHEILA grabs the stroller, and SHE, ROBBIE, and HARVEY exit.)

SHEILA. (*To Robbie as THEY go off.*) New Rochelle: That's where Dick Van Dyke lives ...

(MUSIC intro, and new slide:)

[Music Cue #18: HERE'S TO THE CRABGRASS]

HE MOVES

(During the following song, BARRY and SARAH pull off their hospital gowns, and dispose of them, replacing them with suburban barbecue outfits. BARRY has an apron which says "Daddy's Cookin' Now." THEY march to the intro MUSIC, and a red-checked picnic table is pushed on.)

("Country Gardens")

BARRY.
HERE'S TO THE CRABGRASS
HERE'S TO THE MORTGAGE
IN FACT, HERE'S TO SUBURBIA
SARAH.
LAY DOWN YOUR BRIEFCASE
FAR FROM THE RAT RACE
WHERE NOTHING CAN DISTURB YA

DID YOU SET THE THERMOSTAT?

BARRY.
NO, I DON'T KNOW WHERE IT'S AT
SARAH
TUESDAY, THE CUB SCOUTS MEET AGAIN
BARRY.
WALK THE DOG AND CUT THE GRASS
SARAH.
TAKE THE KIDS TO DANCING CLASS

BARRY.
ROB'S LITTLE LEAGUE GOT BEAT AGAIN
SARAH.
CAN'T KEEP A MAID HERE
NO MATTER WHAT THEY'RE PAID HERE
THE PLACE HAS BAD PUBLICITY
BARRY.
WHY DID WE MOVE HERE?
SARAH.
DON'T YOU REMEMBER?
BOTH.
TO LIVE IN SWEET SIMPLI-CI-TY

(By the end of the song, THEY reach front and center—now middle-aged. BARRY brandishes a large fork, and the couple strikes a pose out of that famous Grant Wood painting.
After the song, BARRY goes to tend the barbecue. SARAH carries a tray full of food, which SHE hands to him.)

BARRY. (*Placing food on the grill.*) Daddy's cookin'! Daddy's cookin' now!
SARAH. Well, put it all on, Daddy—I just saw the Goldfarbs arrive.
BARRY. We'll never make it. Better send out for some reinforcements.

(A sweet gentleman, MR. GOLDFARB, enters from the other direction with a plate of food.)

GOLDFARB. Hello. Hello.
SARAH. Hi, Fred. Nice to see you. Where's Myrtle?
GOLDFARB. Stationed by the shrimp puffs, as usual. Barry, have you seen my kids?
BARRY. Yeah, they're with my kids.
GOLDFARB. I hope they're not playing ... that game again.

BARRY. Don't worry, Fred. Our son wants to go to medical school.

(GOLDFARB nods in relief. MR. BLOOM, a brusque, no-nonsense man, enters.)

BARRY. Uh-oh, honey. Here's Mr. Bloom. Be nice to him. I'm going to ask him for a raise later.

MR. BLOOM. Hey, Bockman. Nice house. I must be paying you too much.

BARRY. (*Trying to laugh.*) That's a good one, sir ...

MR. BLOOM. By the way, I hope this thing doesn't go too late. I want you to go in to the office for a little while later.

BARRY. Mr. Bloom ... it's a holiday. I have a house full of company.

MR. BLOOM. Of course. You're right, Bockman. *Your* company is just as important as *my* company.

BARRY. I'll be in at five.

MR. BLOOM. (*Slaps his back.*) Thanks.

GOLDFARB. (*Sticks out a hand to Mr. Bloom.*) Hi there, I'm Fred Goldfarb.

(BLOOM is silent.)

GOLDFARB. Barry and Sarah's neighbor ...

MR. BLOOM. That's nice.

(GOLDFARB turns back to Barry and Sarah.)

SARAH. I don't think he's in a very good mood.

BARRY. So much for the raise.

SARAH. I've got an idea. (*Crosses to Mr. Bloom.*) Excuse me, Mr. Bloom ... have you heard from your son?

(BLOOM lights up at the mention.)

SARAH. You must be so proud.

MR. BLOOM. My son! My son! (*Now shaking Goldfarb's hand.*) Hi, how are ya?!

(BLOOM walks forward with GOLDFARB into a spotlight.)

[Music Cue #19: SHINE ON, HARVEY BLOOM]

MR. BLOOM.

MY NAME IS MISTER BLOOM AND I'M FROM NEW ROCHELLE
AND I SING THIS HAPPY TUNE
BECAUSE MY SON THE ASTRONAUT, YOUNG HARVEY BLOOM
HAS LANDED ON THE MOON

(HE stares GOLDFARB out of his spotlight.)

MY WIFE AND I, WE MISS OUR LITTLE HARVEY SO
BACK HERE IN NEW ROCHELLE
THAT EVERY SINGLE NIGHT
IN THE PALE MOONLIGHT
WE WALK OUT ON THE PATIO AND YELL:

SHINE ON, SHINE ON, HARVEY BLOOM
UP IN THE SKY
YOU HAVE BEEN IN ORBIT SINCE
JANUARY, FEBRUARY, JUNE AND JULY
DON'T COME BACK TOO SOON, WE RENTED OUT YOUR ROOM
SO SHINE ON, SHINE ON, HARVEY BLOOM
UP THERE ON THE MOON

WE'LL MISS YOU ON THE HOLIDAYS
THIS YEAR THEY'RE COMING LATER
WE HOPE YOU HAVE A VERY LOVELY SEDER IN

YOUR CRATER
YOUR MOMMA SENT THE ASTRONAUTS SOME CHICKEN SOUP AT SCHOOL
THEY'RE USING IT INSTEAD OF ROCKET FUEL

IF YOU LIKE OUTER SPACE YOU OUGHT TO SEE YOUR SISTER JANET
SHE CAME IN WITH A HAIRDO THAT IS FROM ANOTHER PLANET
YOUR GIRLFRIEND SHIRLEY MISSES YOU
THE AIR FORCE SAID SHE HAD
A TEMPER TANTRUM ON THE LAUNCHING PAD

ALL.
SHINE ON, SHINE ON, HARVEY BLOOM
UP IN THE SKY

MR. BLOOM.
UNDER SEPARATE COVER, I'M SENDING YOU SOME PICKLES
AND A CORNED BEEF ON RYE
YOU BROUGHT BROMO SELTZER WITH YOU, I PRESUME

ALL.
SO DINE ON, DINE ON, HARVEY BLOOM!

MR. BLOOM.
HARVEY BLOOM IS ON THE MOON

ALL.
OH YEAH!

SARAH. *Now,* Barry ... *Now* ...

BARRY. (*Summoning courage, approaches Mr. Bloom.*) Uh, Mr. Bloom. You know, I've been working for you for nearly fifteen years. And ... I need a raise.

MR. BLOOM. Tell you what, Bockman ... I'll think about it.

BARRY. Thank you!

MR. BLOOM. (*A millisecond later:*) No.

(BLOOM goes to the picnic table.
SHEILA JACKMAN enters, carrying ten shopping

bags—including Saks, Bonwit's, Bendel's and four suitcases—Vuitton, of course. SHE starts to sing:)

SHEILA.
WESTCHESTER HADASSAH, I GAVE ALL MY DOUGH ...

(In a hideous Spanish accent.) Ola, familia! Estoy aqui.

SARAH. Hi, Mom.

SHEILA. (*To Sarah and Barry in turn.*) How are you? How are you? *(Face to face with Bloom, same tone:) Who* are you?

SARAH. (*Rushing over.*) Mom! You're late.

SHEILA. I had a lot to carry from the car. (*Looks at Barry.*) And no one to help me.

BARRY. Hi, Sheila.

SARAH. So how was your vacation?

SHEILA. Oh, it was, how they say, excellente! Listen to this ... *(Shows off some vocabulary.)* Gracias, Senor, but pour more, por favor! (Oh, I just love that Mexican language.)

GOLDFARB. You mean Spanish, don't you?

SHEILA. Yes, yes! (*Pulls out a sombrero.*) Or maybe I should say, "Si! Si!"?

(MUSIC begins.)

BARRY. No, no ...

[Music Cue #20: MEXICAN HAT DANCE]

("Mexican Hat Dance")

SHEILA.
OH, AMERICANS DANCE ON A DANCE FLOOR
AND THE SPANIARDS, THEY DANCE ON A TABLE
AND THE RUSSIANS, THEY DANCE ON A SABER

BUT THE MEXICANS DANCE ON THEIR HATS

(The OTHERS use their barbecue implements as percussion instruments.)

SHEILA.
OH, THEY DANCE ON HOT COALS IN CALCUTTA
IN WISCONSIN, THEY DANCE ON FRESH BUTTA
WHICH THEY SQUEEZE FROM ONE COW OR ANUDDA
YES, THE MEXICANS DANCE ON THEIR HATS

(SHEILA begins to distribute "Mexicanized" versions of familiar hats.)

THERE ARE MEXICANS DANCING ON DERBIES
THERE ARE MEXICANS DANCING ON CAPS
THEY JUST THROW THEIR FEDORAS WHEREVER THE FLOOR IS
AND START DOING HORAS AND TAPS

THEY WON'T QUIT
ALL.
THEY WON'T QUIT
SHEILA.
THEY GO ON
ALL.
THEY GO ON
IT'S A MEXICAN CUSTOM TO TAKE HATS AND BUST 'EM
BY DOING A DANCE THEREUPON

OH, THE REASON THEY SHOT PANCHO VILLA
WAS HE DANCED ON HIS MOTHER'S MANTILLA
SHEILA.
AND THE MESSAGE DID NOT REACH GARCIA
ALL.
HE WAS OUT SOMEWHERE DANCING ON HATS

GOLDFARB.
THERE'S A FELLOW IN WEST ACAPULCO
SARAH.
THE MOST ELEGANT MAN YOU COULD MEET
MR. BLOOM.
HE DOES SAMBAS ON HOMBURGS
BARRY.
TO TUNES OF SIG ROMBERG'S
SHEILA.
AND SOMETIMES "THE NUTCRACKER SUITE"
SHEILA/ALL.
SO TAKE CARE (SO TAKE CARE)
SO BEWARE (SO BEWARE)
ALL.
OR THEY'LL PUT CASTANETS ON AND RUIN YOUR STETSON
'CAUSE THEY ALL THINK THEY'RE FRED ASTAIRE

(A little DANCE in which the OTHERS get carried away, and Sheila's hat somehow becomes a maypole. Appropriate Latin expressions are called out: "Ole, Xavier Cugat, taco, Juan Peron, etc.")

ALL.
HEY!

(Silence. MR. BLOOM has ended up on top of Sheila's hat.)

SHEILA. *(Shooing him.)*
HEY!

(HE moves.)

ALL.
HEY!

SHEILA.
IF YOU'RE—
SARAH/GOLDFARB.
—EVER IN MEXICO PROPER
SHEILA.
AND YOU'RE—
MR. BLOOM/BARRY.
—WEARING A STRAW HAT OR TOPPER
SHEILA.
WHEN THE—
OTHERS.
—BAND STARTS TO PLAY, CALL A COPPER
MR. BLOOM.
'CAUSE BY NOW YOU SHOULD KNOW
GOLDFARB.
THAT THEY'LL GRAB YOUR CHAPEAU
BARRY.
AND THEY'LL STOMP 'TIL IT'S FLAT
SARAH.
AND THAT'S THAT
SHEILA.
THAT'S WHAT MEXICANS
ALL.
MEXICANS ... MEXICANS ... MEXICANS ... MEXICANS
DO ON YOUR HAT
SHEILA.
OY VEY!

(SHE hands BARRY the rest of her bags.)

SARAH. So, Mom, what do you want to do while you're here?

SHEILA. Well, there are a few good friends I have to visit —(*As SHE and SARAH exit.*) Bergdorf Goodman ... John Wannamaker ... Robert Hall ...

(THEY are gone.)

BARRY. Wow! Sure is a lot of luggage for just a weekend visit. One little weekend and an awful lot of luggage to bring. A visit of two, three days at the tops. All this luggage. Bags. Weekend.

(BELL-TONE, and a SPOTLIGHT of recognition on BARRY, as HE moans.)

BARRY.
IT'S VERY CLEAR ...
HER MOTHER'S HERE TO STAY

(BARRY exits with the suitcases, leaving GOLDFARB and MR. BLOOM.)

GOLDFARB. Great party, isn't it? The desserts are delicious.

MR. BLOOM. (*Looking out front.*) Your wife seems to be enjoying them.

GOLDFARB. (*Looks adoringly.*) Yes, she is. Look at her, just look at her ...

MR. BLOOM. You can't miss her ...

(HE exits, leaving GOLDFARB.)

[Music Cue #21: GROW, MRS. GOLDFARB]

("Glow, Little Glowworm")

GOLDFARB.
GROW, MRS. GOLDFARB, FATTER, FATTER
PILE THE POTATOES ON YOUR PLATTER
LISTEN TO ME 'CAUSE I'M YOUR HUBBY
I JUST ADORE YOU PLUMP AND CHUBBY
I GOT A LETTER FROM THE STATE, DEAR
YOU'RE GONNA NEED A LICENSE PLATE, DEAR
MY LITTLE ELEPHANT JOKE COME TRUE

CHEW, MRS. GOLDFARB, CHEW

THERE IS SO MUCH MORE OF YOU
MORE TO ADORE OF YOU
'CAUSE YOU'RE NOT SLENDER
IN YOUR WHITE DRESS YOU'RE A DOLL
BIG AS THE TAJ MAHAL IN ALL ITS SPLENDOR

WHEN YOU'RE IN DEPARTMENT STORES
DON'T USE REVOLVING DOORS
YOU MIGHT GET STUCK, DEAR
WHEN YOU USE THE TELEPHONE
GO IN THE BOOTH ALONE
AND LOTS OF LUCK, DEAR

YOU HAD FOR BREAKFAST TWO POUNDS BACON
THREE DOZEN EGGS, ONE COFFEE CAKE AND
THEN YOU HAD SOMETHING REALLY AWFUL
FOUR KIPPERED HERRINGS ON A WAFFLE
NINE ENGLISH MUFFINS, ONE BAKED APPLE
BOSTON CREAM PIE, PHILADELPHIA SCRAPPLE
SEVENTEEN BOWLS OF CRISPY CRUNCH
THEN YOU SAID, "WHAT'S FOR LUNCH?"

SWEETHEART, YOU ARE GIANT SIZE
YOU ARE LANE BRYANT SIZE, MY DARLING MYRTLE
LAST THANKSGIVING, I WAS THRILLED
YOU ATE SO MUCH YOU KILLED YOUR LIVING GIRDLE
HAVE ANOTHER DOZEN SHRIMP, MY LOVELY LITTLE BLIMP
DON'T COUNT A CALORIE
I HAVE JUST RECEIVED A STUB
I OWE THE DINER'S CLUB A WHOLE YEAR'S SALARY

EAT, MRS. GOLDFARB, DAILY, NIGHTLY,
EAT, THOUGH YOUR CHAIR IS BENDING SLIGHTLY
LOVE OF MY LIFE, I'M GLAD I FOUND YOU
EACH DAY I TAKE A WALK AROUND YOU
I CAN'T FORGET WHEN WE WERE MARRIED
OVER THE THRESHOLD I GOT CARRIED
NO OTHER BRIDE WAS E'ER SO SWEET
EAT, MRS. GOLDFARB, EAT!

BLACKOUT

[Music Cue #21A: Scene Change 4]

(When the LIGHTS come up, SARAH and SHEILA enter, armed and ready for an exhaustive day of shopping.)

SHEILA. Sarah—I can't believe you were going to buy those shoes!

SARAH. Mom, they were comfortable. They were stylish.

SHEILA. They were retail! (*Looks to the Heavens; shakes head.*) But I'm not going to worry, because you're going to learn. See, shopping, shopping is in your blood. Did I ever tell you that I went into labor with you at a clearance sale?

SARAH. Yes, you did. That's why my middle name is "Filene."

SHEILA. Don't complain. An hour earlier and you would have been Sy Syms.

(Across the way, "ROSE" enters, ready for the sale.)

ROSE. I'm tired of shopping, Mother, I want to go home and do my nails.

(SHIRLEY, her "MOTHER," enters.)

SHIRLEY. You can clip your cuticles anytime, dear, this is a once in a lifetime sale. Besides, you want to get a dress for the Prom, don't you?

ROSE. Oh, who cares? No one is going to ask me.

SHIRLEY. Those boys are just jealous—you winning that shot put competition. I hate when you fret. A beautiful young thing like you.

ROSE. Well, I don't *feel* very beautiful.

SHIRLEY. *(Holding Rose's face.)* You are beautiful. You are. (*Pause.*) You could use a shave, but you're beautiful ....

(A STORE MANAGER enters, pushing a table of sale items.)

STORE MANAGER. The store is about to open.

(ROSE and SHIRLEY collide with SHEILA and SARAH on their way to the sale.)

SHEILA. Excuse me.

SHIRLEY. You're excused.

ROSE. Mommy. These ladies are ahead of us.

SHIRLEY. No, I think we were here first. You don't mind, do you, hon?

SHEILA. *(Stares at her.)* I've got two words for you, darling ... LEG WAX.

(THEY'RE about to go at it:)

STORE MANAGER. Shoppers, take your positions.

(The WOMEN take race-starting positions, and the STORE MANAGER becomes a square dance caller, speaking to the MUSIC.)

[Music Cue #22: JUMP DOWN, SPIN AROUND]

("Jump Down, Spin Around")

STORE MANAGER.
CURTSEY TO YOUR NEIGHBOR AND WAVE HELLO
READY, SHOPPERS—HERE WE GO!

GOTTA JUMP DOWN SPIN AROUND AND PICK A DRESS OF COTTON
GOTTA JUMP DOWN SPIN AROUND AND PICK A DRESS OF WOOL
GOTTA JUMP DOWN SPIN AROUND AND PICK A DRESS OF COTTON
GOTTA JUMP DOWN SPIN AROUND AND PICK A DRESS OF WOOL
ALL.
GRAB THOSE BARGAINS OFF THOSE RACKS
WHO NEEDS BERGDORF'S? WHO NEEDS SAKS?
STORE MANAGER.
GOTTA JUMP DOWN SPIN AROUND AND PICK A DRESS OF COTTON
GOTTA JUMP DOWN (BOOM)—PICK A DRESS OF WOOL

NOW MOSEY ON DOWN TO CHAT WITH YOUR KIN
TELL 'EM WHAT YOU BOUGHT—THEN DO IT AGIN
GRAB YOUR PARTNER—GRAB YOUR PURSE
PROMENADE, BUT IN REVERSE

GOTTA JUMP DOWN SPIN AROUND AND SAVE A DOLLAR EIGHTY
GOTTA JUMP DOWN SPIN AROUND AND SAVE A LOTTA DOUGH

GOTTA JUMP DOWN SPIN AROUND AND SAVE A DOLLAR EIGHTY
GOTTA JUMP DOWN SPIN AROUND AND SAVE A LOTTA DOUGH

ALL.

HERE'S WHAT I'VE BEEN SEARCHING FOR
A GENU-INE COPY OF A FAKE DIOR

STORE MANAGER.

GOTTA JUMP DOWN SPIN AROUND AND SAVE A DOLLAR EIGHTY
GOTTA JUMP DOWN (BOOM)—SAVE A LOTTA DOUGH
ATTENTION LADIES—SALE ON FOUR
TAKE THE STAIRS OR THE ESCALA-TOR
NO MATTER WHAT YOUR INCOME—
NO MATTER WHAT YOUR SEX
WE TAKE CASH OR TRAVELLER'S CHECKS

TRY ON BLOUSES FOR A WHILE
THEN SLIP ON SHOES IN ANOTHER AISLE
FIND A JACKET TO GO WITH 'EM
SHOP 'TIL YOU DROP, BUT DO IT IN RHYTHM

(HE leads a slap dance.)

EV'RYBODY, DO-SI-DO
READY, SET—HERE WE GO!

(THEY all do the slap dance.)

COME ON, PEOPLE, DON'T HESITATE
TIME'S A WASTIN', IT'S GETTIN' LATE
WE CLOSE AT NINE, AND DON'T FORGET
YOU GOT THREE MORE FLOORS TO GO THROUGH YET

GOTTA JUMP DOWN SPIN AROUND AND PICK A DRESS OF COTTON

GOTTA JUMP DOWN SPIN AROUND AND PICK A DRESS OF WOOL
GOTTA JUMP DOWN SPIN AROUND AND PICK A DRESS OF COTTON
GOTTA JUMP DOWN SPIN AROUND AND PICK A DRESS OF WOOL

SHEILA.
SEE HOW THIS ONE LOOKS ON ME

SARAH.
JUST LIKE JACKIE KENNEDY

STORE MANAGER.
GOTTA JUMP DOWN SPIN AROUND AND PICK A DRESS OF COTTON
GOTTA JUMP DOWN SPIN AROUND AND PICK A DRESS OF WOOL

SHIRLEY.
HERE'S A SIZE EIGHT I COULD FIX

ROSE.
BETTA LET IT OUT TO A FORTY-SIX

STORE MANAGER.
GOTTA JUMP DOWN SPIN AROUND AND TAKE IT OFF A RACK
GOTTA JUMP DOWN SPIN AROUND AND TRY IT ON YOUR BACK

(A fight breaks out amongst the SHOPPERS.)

STORE MANAGER.
LITTLE SHIRLEY JUMP DOWN
TOOK ONE OFF A HANGER
LITTLE SHEILA JUMP DOWN
GRABBED IT AWAY
LITTLE ROSE JUMP DOWN
LITTLE SARAH JUMP DOWN
ROSE, SHEILA, SARAH, SHIRLEY
REMEMBER, LADIES, WE'RE CLOSIN' EARLY!

GOTTA JUMP DOWN (WHOOP) TAKE IT OFF A

HANGER
GOTTA JUMP DOWN (WHOOP WHOOP) GRAB IT RIGHT AWAY

OH PICK A DRESS OF COTTON

ALL.
OH PICK A DRESS OF WOOL

STORE MANAGER.
OH THAT'S THE WAY IT GOES

ALL.
OH WHAT A SALE OF CLOTHES

STORE MANAGER.
GOTTA JUMP DOWN (WHOOP) PICK A DRESS OF COTTON
GOTTA JUMP DOWN (WHOOP WHOOP) PICK A DRESS OF WOOL

IT'S CLOSIN' TIME—GOTTA STOP RIGHT HERE
SO TAKE YOUR BAGS AND PAY THE CASHIER
YOU WANNA EXCHANGE? JUST BRING THE RECEIPT
I'M SORRY, FOLKS—BUT MOVE YOUR FEET
COME BACK REAL SOON—TAKE MY ADVICE
THE WHOLE DAMN STORE WILL BE HALF PRICE!

(With no more sale clothes, the SHOPPERS eye the STORE MANAGER maniacally, chanting rhythmically. THEY approach him and pull his shirt off.)

STORE MANAGER. Ladies! Please! That's not for sale!!

(THEY rip off his pants.)

BLACKOUT

[Music Cue #22A: JUMP DOWN – Playoff]

HE IS OLDER

(In the DARK, on tape, SARAH reads a letter to her mother. SLIDES show the exterior of a comfortable suburban home at night, a LIGHT on in one upstairs window:)

SARAH. *(V.O.)* "Hi Mom,

This is your daughter—the one who didn't marry the dentist or dermatologist.

Barry and I want to thank you for your anniversary gift—the new furniture for the guest room looks great. I hope *you* like it, since you live there nine months out of the year.

The trip to Brazil sounds like fun; that photo you sent is breathtaking. Leave it to you to find the only Loehmann's in the Amazon.

Your grandchildren are growing so fast. Sophie is dating the captain of the football team ... the captain of the baseball team ... and the captain of the USS Montgomery anchored nearby.

And Robbie is starting college. Again.

Barry just got another promotion, so he's working harder than ever. If Daddy were still here, he would be so proud of him. (*Beat.*) He wouldn't know what to call him, but he would be proud of him.

(The LIGHTS come up on SARAH and BARRY in bed. BARRY is sleeping, but SARAH sits up writing.)

SARAH. Well, that's all for now. Barry just told me to send his love.

Miss you, Mom.

Your daughter,

Sarah Filene Jackman Bockman."

(INTRO music starts, and SARAH nudges BARRY who grunts.)

SARAH. Barry ... Barry ... are you sleeping?!

BARRY. (*Annoyed.*) No ... I'm doing my taxes.

SARAH. (*Still nudging.*) It's three a.m. Sophie didn't come home yet ... (*Sings.*)

[Music Cue #23: CRAZY DOWNTOWN]

("Downtown")

MOMMY AND DAD ARE NEVER NERVOUS OR MAD
WHEN THE TEENAGERS GO ... DOWNTOWN
DADDY AND MOM JUST STAY AT HOME AND KEEP CALM
AND WATCH "THE LATE LATE SHOW" ... UPTOWN

'CAUSE WHEN THE KIDS ARE GONE WE GET TO SPEND SOME TIME ALONE HERE
THAT'S OUR ONLY CHANCE TO USE THE BATHTUB AND THE PHONE HERE
WHEN THEY'RE AWAY

BESIDES WE'RE STUCK WHERE WE ARE
BECAUSE THE KIDS TOOK OUR MONEY
THE KIDS TOOK OUR CAR AND WENT
DOWNTOWN—WHERE COULD THEY POSSIBLY...?
DOWNTOWN—IT'S TWENTY AFTER THREE
DOWNTOWN—WHY DOESN'T SOMEBODY CALL?

Barry, was that the phone?

(BARRY grunts.)

SARAH.
THEY DON'T COME HOME TILL FOUR A.M.
'CAUSE THEY'RE ROAMING IN THE STREETS SOMEWHERE

BARRY. (*In his sleep.*)
DOWNTOWN

SARAH.
WE WOULD FEEL SWELL IF ONLY SOMEONE WOULD TELL US WHAT GOES ON DOWN THERE

BARRY.
DOWNTOWN

SARAH.
BUT EVERY TIME WE ASK THEM WHAT THEY'RE DOING AFTER DARK THERE
THEY JUST SAY THAT THEY ARE LOOKING FOR PETULA CLARK THERE
WHAT DOES THAT MEAN?

SO, KIDS, GIVE YOUR FOLKS A BREAK
BECAUSE YOU'RE DRIVING US CRAZY
YOU KEEP US AWAKE, WE TAKE

MIL-TOWN—SWALLOWING PILLS SO WE'LL
CALM DOWN—COUNTING THE HOURS YOU'RE
DOWNTOWN—OH, GOD, IT'S TWENTY TO FOUR

(MUSIC continues.)

SARAH. (*Nudging Barry.*) Barry! Wake up. I'm worried about Sophie.

BARRY. Just calm down. What's the worst that could happen to her?

(And now, as MUSIC plays, we see Sarah's worst fantasy visualize across the stage.
SOPHIE enters, in wild party clothes, laughing drunkenly.

A LEATHER BIKER swaggers out, chugs a beer, and belches, while SHE laughs. THEY start to make out.
SARAH, in her bathrobe, has joined her own nightmare, looking on, trying to get their attention.
Oblivious, SOPHIE indicates to the BIKER that she is pregnant, and, immediately HE heads out of town. Now, SOPHIE looks for a hand-out, and with no luck, pulls a gun.
Sound of a SIREN. A POLICEMAN enters, and handcuffs SOPHIE, leading her out.
SARAH is now discovered back in bed, horrified.)

SARAH.
WHILE WE'RE LYING HERE WE TRY TO WATCH THE TELEVISION
THEN THEY CALL US UP AND SAY THEY'VE HAD A SLIGHT COLLISION

THERE GOES THE CAR

BESIDE THAT, THEY'VE BEEN ARRESTED
SO WE'VE GOT TO GET UP AND
WE'VE GOT TO GET DRESSED
AND GO—

(BARRY automatically rises, half-asleep, singing:)

SARAH/BARRY.
DOWNTOWN
SARAH.
BORROW A CAR AND GO
SARAH/BARRY.
DOWNTOWN
SARAH.
THAT'S WHERE THEY ARE
THEY WENT
SARAH/BARRY.
DOWNTOWN

SARAH.
WAIT TILL WE GET THAT KID HOME

(While SARAH rants and raves, SOPHIE appears in her nightgown.)

SOPHIE. Hey, what's all the noise? Can't a person get any sleep in this house?

SARAH. Darling, what are you—? I thought you were out.

SOPHIE. I got home from band practice hours ago. Mom, is something wrong?

(BARRY immediately heads back to bed, and goes to sleep.)

SARAH. No, no ... you know how your father worries. Good night, darling.

SOPHIE. 'Night, Mom, Dad. (*Exits.*)

SARAH. Well, that's a relief.

(SARAH puts her head down. A MALE VOICE is heard offstage.)

VOICE. (*O.S.*) Hey, baby, what took so long?

(Sounds of SOPHIE's giggles O.S. As the last beat of the song sounds, BARRY and SARAH sit up, eyes wide open.)

BARRY. Sarah, did you hear something?

SARAH. Oh, I hope not.

BARRY. I'm going to the office. Bloom wants me in early anyway.

SARAH. Not this early. Come back to bed.

(HE sits down.)

SARAH. Barry, what's wrong?

BARRY. What's wrong? I have terrible indigestion. My boss is killing me. The mortgage is impossible. The new roof is leaking. The old furnace is broken. And my son is a Hare Krishna.

SARAH. At least he plays an instrument ... (*Gets an idea, and pats the pillow, sexily.*) Oh, well. I know what you need ... (*SHE begins to fondle him.*)

BARRY. (*Pulling away.*) I need *sleep*.

SARAH. (*Annoyed.*) It always put you to sleep before ...

BARRY. I gotta get dressed.

(SHE reaches for him, but HE exits.)

SARAH. Barry … (*Sings sadly.*)
BARRY BOCKMAN, BARRY BOCKMAN
WHERE ARE YOU?...

(FADE OUT. Then, LIGHTS up on:
BARRY, in his bathrobe, staring into the bathroom mirror, checking his growing bald spot. HE shaves, and sings:)

[Music Cue #24: DID I EVER REALLY LIVE?]

("Did I Every Really Live?")

BARRY.
YOU'RE BORN, YOU WEEP
YOU SMILE, YOU SLEEP
YOU CLING, YOU CRAWL
YOU STAND, YOU FALL
YOU STAND AGAIN AND TRY
AND THEN YOU WALK
YOU EAT, YOU DRINK
YOU FEEL, YOU THINK
YOU PLAY, YOU GROW

YOU LEARN, YOU KNOW
AND THEN ONE DAY—
  YOU FIND A WAY TO TALK

YOU'RE YOUNG, YOU FLY
YOU LAUGH, YOU CRY
YOU'RE GROWN,
  YOU'RE ON YOUR OWN AT LAST
YOU LOSE, YOU WIN
YOUR DAYS BEGIN
TO SLIP AWAY TOO FAST ... TOO FAST

TOO SOON YOU'LL HEAR A DISTANT DRUM
TOO SOON THE TIME TO GO WILL COME
AND TIME WON'T WAIT—IS IT TOO LATE TO ASK
DID I EVER LOVE?
DID I EVER GIVE?
DID I EVER REALLY LIVE?

(Underscoring continues, and a VOICE booms out:)

VOICE. *(V.O.)* Questions, questions, questions—what is this, "Jeopardy"?

BARRY. Hunh!? What's that? Who are you? God?

(The VOICE materializes—a MAN with wings, halo, and a polyester tuxedo. It's PHIL, singing.)

PHIL. *(Sings.)*
HEAVEN, I'M IN HEAVEN ...
Thank you!!

BARRY. You're not God ... you're Uncle Phil!

PHIL. I have come from the great beyond to deliver an eternal message: "Cheer up." G'bye.

BARRY. That's the whole message?

PHIL. Yes, that's the whole message. Why?

BARRY. I don't know. Such a long trip ...

PHIL. Okay. Try this one. *(Grandly.)* "Live what

you live. Love what you love. Do what you do."

BARRY. (*Transfixed.*) What do you mean?

PHIL. I have absolutely no idea.

BARRY. Wait, I know what you mean. You mean—a person should make the most of whatever life he has. Cherish those who are close to him, and learn to deal with the rest. Right?

PHIL. (*Not quite paying attention.*) Hunh? Whatever. So, go back in the other room. Take that little kneidle of mine, give her a big kiss and ... Noah, hit it!

(HARP music intro.)

BARRY. Noah, the band leader from my wedding?

PHIL. Nah. Noah ... from the Ark. So go and take your wife in your arms, and: (*Sings.*)

[Music Cue #24A: HELLO MUDDAH,
HELLO FADDUH! - Reprise]

TELL HER, "SARAH—THIS IS BARRY
YOU'RE THE ONLY GIRL I'D MARRY"
TELL HER, "LET'S GO BACK TO BED NOW
SO THAT UNCLE PHIL CAN GO BACK AND BE DEAD NOW ..."

Thank you!

(PHIL disappears.
LIGHTS come up on SARAH in bed. BARRY runs on, and playfully jumps on the bed.)

BARRY. Sarah!

SARAH. Barry?! What are you doing? I thought you were going to the office.

BARRY. No ... I didn't go. I was talking to Phil.

SARAH. Phil Solomon, your lawyer?

BARRY. No, no, *Uncle* Phil. The dead one.

SARAH. Barry, are you sick?
BARRY. Sarah, you look beautiful.
SARAH. Now I know you're sick.
BARRY. No, I mean it. I'm not sick. I feel ... great!

(HE leans over and gives her a kiss.)

SARAH. (*Embarrassed.*) Barry, come on ... we can't now ... Barry, stop ...

(BARRY playfully pursues her across, and then around the bed, barking and the like.
Finally, SARAH turns sharply.)

SARAH. Hold on, Mr. Sweet Talk. When you don't start your car engine for a few months, it doesn't just turn over right away ...

(MUSIC intro, while BARRY blocks SARAH from walking off.)

[Music Cue #25: LIKE YOURS]

("Like Yours")

BARRY.
HAVE I EVER SEEN EYES LIKE YOURS?
HAVE I EVER SEEN LIPS LIKE YOURS?
HAVE I EVER TOUCHED CHEEKS OR HEARD AN ANGEL'S VOICE
THAT SPEAKS LIKE YOURS?
MAY LIGHTNING STRIKE ME
MAY I SINK THROUGH THE FLOOR
IF I'VE EVER SEEN THINGS LIKE YOURS ON ANY GIRL BEFORE

WOULD I LIE ABOUT EYES LIKE YOURS?
WOULD I LIE ABOUT LIPS LIKE YOURS?

DO YOU THINK THAT I'M CAPABLE OF LYING 'BOUT
A SHAPE LIKE YOURS?
MAY I FALL IN A FAINT
MAY I SIT IN WET PAINT
MAY I STEP ON A MANHOLE
WHERE THE COVER JUST AIN'T
IF I'VE EVER SEEN EYES AND LIPS THE WAY YOU GOT 'EM
AND CHARMS LIKE YOURS FROM TOP TO BOTTOM
AND ALL THOSE BEAUTIFUL THINGS LIKE YOURS

SARAH.

IF I'D NEVER HEARD WORDS LIKE YOURS
IF I'D NEVER HEARD TALK LIKE YOURS
I WOULD THINK IT'S DIVINE WHEN SOMEONE HANDED ME A LINE LIKE YOURS
MAY I LOSE MY BIKINI
MAY I BREAK ALL MY NAILS
IF I HAVEN'T HEARD THINGS THAT SOUND MORE TRUE
IN FAIRY TALES

HAVE I EVER HEARD LIES LIKE YOURS
COMING OUT OF A MOUTH LIKE YOURS?
HAVE I HEARD AN AMAZING LIST OF TIRED OLD CLICHES LIKE YOURS?
MAY MY MAIL BE ALL BILLS
MAY I SUFFER FROM CHILLS

(*Spoken.*) Barry, stop, I'm getting a hot flash!

BARRY. Menopause becomes you!

SARAH. Barry!

(Sings.)

IF I EVER MET ANYONE AS FAKE AND PHONEY

BARRY.
AND FULL OF SHALL WE SAY BALONEY
BOTH.
AND OTHER BEAUTIFUL THINGS LIKE YOURS
OTHER BEAUTIFUL THINGS LIKE YOURS!

(SARAH beckons sexily for Barry to come to bed.)

SARAH. Oh, Barry ... you're an angel.
BARRY. *(Looks up toward Phil in Heaven.)* Thank you!!

BLACKOUT

[Music Cue #25A: Scene Change 5]

HE IS OLD

(A beach. A sign, "BEACH CLOSED—MIAMI BEACH POLICE." An elderly COUPLE, NAT and DORIS, sit on a bench. DORIS is sunning with a reflector. LENNY, another old guy, sits near them. THEY wear loud shirts and sun hats, and read the Miami paper.)

NAT. Oy.
DORIS. Oy, what?
NAT. What do you mean, oy, what?
DORIS. "Oy" your back, or "Oy" your leg?
NAT. "Oy" in general.
DORIS. Did I tell you that Cousin Sy is getting remarried?
NAT. Yes, you told me already.
DORIS. Did I tell you the children called?
NAT. Yes, you told me that, too! Why do you keep repeating yourself?!

(Pause.)

DORIS. Did I tell you that Cousin Sy is getting remarried?

(Pause.)

NAT. (*Interested.*) Really? To who?

(Pause.)

DORIS. I don't remember.
LENNY. (*Seeing something in the paper.*) Look, Harry Lewis died.
DORIS. (*Gets very upset.*) Oh, no!!! Ohhhhhhh! *(Then:)* Who's Harry Lewis?
LENNY. I don't know. It just says that thing here.
DORIS. I don't read the paper anymore. It depresses me. Everything is sex, sex and more sex.

(LENNY and NAT agree. Pause.)

LENNY. Where do you *get* that paper?
DORIS. It's not like the old days ... (*Sings.*)

[Music Cue #26: DOWN THE DRAIN]

THE SWEETEST THINGS IN LIFE
DON'T STAY AROUND FOR VERY LONG
THEY COME AND GO AND DON'T COME BACK AGAIN
MEN. (*Barbershop style.*)
COME BACK AGAIN
DORIS.
WHILE THEY'RE HERE YOU FEEL SO SMUG
THAT'S WHEN FATE PULLS OUT THE PLUG
AND THE SWEETEST THINGS IN LIFE
GO DOWN THE DRAIN

MEN.
GO DOWN THE DRAIN

(THEY rise, painfully, and inch their walkers to stage center.)

NAT.
WHAT HAS HAPPENED TO GOLASHES?
LENNY.
DOWN THE DRAIN
NAT/DORIS.
DOWN THE DRAIN
LENNY.
WHERE'S THE CZAR OF ALL THE RUSSIAS?
DORIS.
DOWN THE DRAIN
MEN.
DOWN THE DRAIN
DORIS.
WHERE'S THE FIVE-CENT CANDY BAR?
NAT.
AND THE GOOD OLD EDSEL CAR?
LENNY.
GONE WHERE ALL THE SWELL THINGS ARE
ALL.
DOWN (DOWN) (DOWN) THE DRAIN
WHERE ARE TELEPHONE PREFIXES?
LENNY.
DOWN THE DRAIN
DORIS/NAT.
DOWN THE DRAIN
ALL.
THEY'VE ALL GONE TO WHERE TOM MIX IS
DORIS.
DOWN THE DRAIN
MEN.
RIGHT DOWN THE DRAIN

NAT.
WHERE'S THOSE GRAND OLD GOLD DUST TWINS?
LENNY.
ALL THOSE GERMAN ZEPPELINS
DORIS.
BOYS WHO SET UP BOWLING PINS
ALL.
DOWN (DOWN) (DOWN) THE DRAIN
SUPPOSE WE MADE A FUSS ABOUT THE DOUBLE-DECKER BUS
DO YOU SUPPOSE THEY'D BRING IT BACK AGAIN?
DORIS.
FOUNTAIN PENS THAT USE REAL INK
LENNY.
COINS THAT DON'T GO "CLUNK" BUT "CLINK"
NAT.
THE THINGS WE LOVE ARE SINKING
ALL.
DOWN THE DRAIN
RIGHT DOWN THE DRAIN

WHERE ARE ALL THOSE KAMIKAZES?
DOWN THE DRAIN, DOWN THE DRAIN
AND THE HOTEL SAVOY PLAZ-YS?
DOWN THE DRAIN, RIGHT DOWN THE DRAIN
NAT.
WHERE'S THE NEW YORK WORLD'S FAIR?
DORIS.
I JUST SAW IT STANDING THERE
LENNY.
IN THE HEART OF FLUSHING—
NAT/DORIS.
WHERE?
LENNY.
FLUSHING!

NAT/DORIS.
OH!
ALL.
FLUSHING—DOWN THE DRAIN

NAT. Here come Barry and Sarah Bockman. Such nice people. Look, they bought their shirts at K-Mart, too.

(An elderly BARRY and SARAH enter. THEY are wearing loud shirts, as well. BARRY carries the paper.)

BARRY. Hello, Lenny. Hello, Nat, Doris. How are you?
DORIS. Oy.
SARAH. Oy, it's hot? Oy, it's cold?
NAT. General Oy.

(The BOCKMANS sit.)

BARRY. It *is* hot.
SARAH. Well, that's why we moved to Florida: Because of the weather ... and the grandchildren.
NAT. I thought your grandchildren were in New York?
SARAH. (*Beat.*) That's right ... That reminds me. Look who wrote to us ... *(SHE pulls out a postcard and hands it to BARRY; explains to others.)* Our grandson went away for the first time this summer. To Camp Granada.

(ALL sigh.)

LENNY. I miss being a kid, at camp.
DORIS. Now, everything is different. We grow a little older ... a little wiser ... a little fatter ... (*Begins to sing.*)

ANATEVKA, ANATEVKA

NAT. *(Interrupts.)* Excuse Doris, she just did "Fiddler" at the Sisterhood.

BARRY. *(Opens up his paper and reads:)* Oh, no.

SARAH. What's the matter?

BARRY. Nothing.

SARAH. I hate it when he does that. Come on, bubbala, let's go eat.

BARRY. *(Depressed.)* I don't feel like eating. Maybe later.

SARAH. We can't go later. The Early Bird Special closes at four, and we have a reservation.

BARRY. I don't feel like eating at four. I don't feel like anything.

SARAH. Barry, what is it?

BARRY. Harry Lewis died.

DORIS. *(Despondent.)* Again?!!

SARAH. Who's Harry Lewis?

LENNY. A person who died.

SARAH. What did he do?

BARRY. It says here he "sold fabric." How tragic. You live a whole life, and it's summed up in two words. Sold. Fabric.

NAT. Two words can never sum up a person's life!

DORIS. "Fixed toilets." *(Looks at Nat.)* Works for you.

NAT. Thanks.

BARRY. I'm depressed.

DORIS. Me, too.

(THEY are all depressed.)

SARAH. Now hold on, everybody. *(MUSIC starts.)* I didn't know Harry Lewis, but I'm sure he did more than sell fabric. I'm sure in his own way, to his own family, Harry Lewis was as big a hero as anybody. *(Sings:)*

[Music Cue #27: THE BALLAD OF HARRY LEWIS]

("Battle Hymn of the Republic")

I'M SINGING YOU THE BALLAD OF A GREAT MAN OF THE CLOTH
HIS NAME WAS HARRY LEWIS AND HE WORKED FOR ...

(Reads in Barry's paper.)

... IRVING ROTH

HE DIED WHILE CUTTING VELVET ON A HOT JULY THE FOURTH
BUT HIS CLOTH GOES SHINING ON

GLORY, GLORY, HARRY LEWIS
GLORY, GLORY, HARRY LEWIS
GLORY, GLORY, HARRY LEWIS
HIS CLOTH GOES SHINING ON

(Newly inspired, ALL but BARRY rise as THEY sing.)

LENNY.
OH, HARRY LEWIS PERISHED IN THE SERVICE OF HIS LORD
HE WAS TRAMPLING THROUGH THE WAREHOUSE WHERE THE DRAPES OF ROTH ARE STORED
NAT.
HE HAD THE FINEST FUNERAL—
NAT/DORIS.
THE UNION COULD AFFORD
TRIO AND SARAH.
HIS CLOTH GOES SHINING ON

GLORY, GLORY, HARRY LEWIS

GLORY, GLORY, HARRY LEWIS
GLORY, GLORY, HARRY LEWIS
HIS CLOTH GOES SHINING ON

(Finally, BARRY rises with renewed hope. The OTHERS remove their hats and sing "oo.")

BARRY.
ALTHOUGH THE FIRE WAS RAGING
HARRY STOOD BY HIS MACHINE
AND WHEN THE FIREMEN BROKE IN
THEY DISCOVERED HIM BETWEEN
A PILE OF ROASTED DACRON
AND SOME FRENCH-FRIED GABARDINE
ALL.
HIS CLOTH GOES SHINING ON

GLORY, GLORY, HARRY LEWIS
GLORY, GLORY, HARRY LEWIS
GLORY, GLORY, HARRY LEWIS
HIS CLOTH GOES SHINING ON!

(Truly rejuvenated, the GROUP performs gymnastic feats, and sings flashy vocal counterpoint.)

GLORY, GLORY, HARRY LEWIS
GLORY, GLORY, HARRY LEWIS
GLORY, GLORY, HARRY LEWIS
HIS CLOTH GOES SHINING—

(A BRIGHT LIGHT suddenly shines over them. A booming voice is heard:)

VOICE. (*V.O.*) Bockman, party of five, your table is waiting.

(THEY all look to each other. SARAH offers her hand to Barry.)

SARAH. Barry?...
BARRY. (*Taking her hand.*) I'm ready.

(THEY smile, and the GROUP marches toward the light.)

ALL.
ON! AND ON! AND ON! AND ON!
AND ON!

(As the LIGHTS fade, THEY form a tableau in silhouette.)

BLACKOUT

[Music Cue #8: BOWS]

THEY MEDLEY

[Music Cue #29: MEDLEY]

("Jimmy Crack Corn")

MAN 1.
OH, SALESMEN COME AND SALESMEN GO
AND MY BEST ONE IS GONE I KNOW
AND IF HE DON'T COME BACK TO ME
I'LL HAVE TO CLOSE THE FACTORY
ALL.
GIMME JACK COHEN AND I DON'T CARE!
GIMME JACK COHEN AND I DON'T CARE!
GIMME JACK COHEN AND I DON'T CARE!
MAN 1.
BUT THE BASTARD'S GONE AWAY!

("God Rest Ye, Merry Gentlemen")

WOMAN 1/MAN 2.
GOD BLESS YOU, JERRY MENDELBAUM
LET NOTHING YOU DISMAY
DIS MAY YOU HAD A ROTTEN MONTH
SO WHAT IS THERE TO SAY
LET'S HOPE NEXT MAY IS BETTER AND GOOD THINGS WILL COME YOUR WAY
AND YOU WON'T HAVE A FEELING OF DISMAY
NEXT MAY

("Camptown Races")

WOMAN 2.
THE CATSKILL LADIES SING THIS SONG
ALL.
HOO HAH! HOO HAH!
WOMAN 2.
SITTING ON THE FRONT PORCH PLAYING MAH-JONG
ALL.
ALL THE HOO HAH DAY!

("The Yellow Rose of Texas")

MAN 3.
OH, I'M MELVIN ROSE OF TEXAS
AND MY FRIENDS ALL CALL ME "TEX"
(**MAN 2.** Hi, Tex!)
WHEN I LIVED IN OLD NEW MEXICO
THEY USED TO CALL ME "MEX"
(**WOMAN 2.** Hey, Mex!)
WHEN I LIVED IN OLD KENTUCKY
THEY CALLED ME "OLD KENTUCK"
(**WOMAN 1.** Kentuck!)
I WAS BORN IN OLD SHAMOKIN WHICH IS

WHY THEY CALL ME "MELVIN ROSE"

("Bye Bye Blackbird")

MEN.
EVERY TIME I FLY AWAY, PEOPLE CRY AND THEY SAY
ALL.
"BYE BYE BLUMBERG"
MEN.
IT'S A SHAME I HAVE TO GO
SEEING AS HOW THEY MISS ME SO
ALL.
"BYE BYE BLUMBERG"

("Second Hand Rose")

WOMEN.
I'M CALLING DR. MAX ROSE
THAT'S WHO I CHOSE
HE'S GONNA MAKE ME A
SECOND HAND NOSE
WOMAN 2.
I WENT TO HIS OFFICE ONCE OR TWICE AND
WOMAN 1.
ALL HIS PATIENTS LOOK LIKE BARBRA STREISAND

("Beautiful Dreamer")

MAN 2.
BEAUTIFUL TEAMSTERS, PLEASE LET ME JOIN
CAN'T DRIVE A TRUCK, BUT I'M WILLING TO LOIN
BEAUTIFUL TEAMSTERS, I'LL PAY THE DUES
GIVE ME THE NEWS THAT I'M NOW ONE OF YOUZE

("Mammy's Little Baby Loves Shortbread")

ALL.
MAMMA'S LITTLE BABY LOVES MATZO, MATZO
MAMMA'S LITTLE BABY LOVES MATZO BALLS
MAMMA'S LITTLE BABY LOVES POTS AND POTS AND
LOTS AND LOTSA MA-TZO ...

("Comin' Through The Rye")

ALL.
DO NOT MAKE A STINGY SANDWICH
PILE THE COLD CUTS HIGH
CUSTOMERS SHOULD SEE SALAMI
COMIN' THROUGH THE RYE

("Down By The Riverside")

ALL.
WHEN YOU GO TO THE DELICATESSEN STORE
DON'T BUY THE LIVERWURST
DON'T BUY THE LIVERWURST
DON'T BUY THE LIVERWURST

IT'LL MAKE YOUR INSIDES AWFULLY SORE
DON'T BUY THE LIVERWURST
DON'T BUY THE LIVERWURST!
MEN.
OH, BUY THE CORNED BEEF IF YOU MUST
THE PICKLED HERRING YOU CAN TRUST
AND THE LOX PUTS YOU IN ORBIT A-OK!
WOMEN.
A-OK!
BUT THAT BIG HUNK OF LIVERWURST
HAS BEEN THERE SINCE OCTOBER FIRST
ALL.
AND TODAY IS THE TWENTY-THIRD OF MAY

SO WHEN YOU GO TO THE DELICATESSEN STORE
DON'T BUY THE LIVERWURST
DON'T BUY THE LIVERWURST
DON'T BUY THE LIVERWURST

I REPEAT WHAT I HAVE SAID BEFORE
DON'T BUY THE LIVERWURST
DON'T BUY THE LIVERWURST!

HIS TRUTH GOES SHINING ON

(Large reproductions of the Allan Sherman record albums are revealed.)

AND ON! AND ON! AND ON! AND ON!

BLACKOUT

[Music Cue #30: Exit Music]

AN ALLAN SHERMAN GLOSSARY

Boychick: an affectionate term of endearment, not an Israeli cross-dresser.

Cantor: the spiritual music leader of a Jewish religious service; what horses do at the Hialeah racetrack.

Flushing: site of 1964 New York World's Fair; what your mother said you never did.

Grand Concourse: large avenue in the Bronx, near Yankee Stadium. (Your grandmother used to live there.)

Grossinger's: a big resort in the Catskills; disgusting sopranos, altos and tenors.

Hadassah: Hebrew for "let's have a luncheon."

Halvah: ethnic candy that crumbles easily. Not to be confused with the fancy-schmancy college in Cambridge, Mass.

New Rochelle: Westchester suburb of New York City, where people can afford to send a kid to that fancy-schmancy college in Cambridge, Mass.

Liverwurst: a cold cut that's been around forever but nobody seems to eat.

Manny Hanny: short for Manufacturers Hanover, a big bank in New York (not an S & L, so it's still there, thank God.)

Noodnik: dum-dum, stupid fellow; a small pasta used in Jewish cooking.

Zetz: Yiddish for "slap"; not to be confused with skin condition of teenagers.

FAVORITE MUSICALS *from*

"The House of Plays"

A FINE AND PRIVATE PLACE

(All Groups) Book & Lyrics by Erik Haagensen. Music by Richard Isen. Adapted from the novel by Peter S. Beagle. 3m., 2f, (may be played by 2m., 2f.) + 1 raven (may be either m. or f.) Ext. setting. "The grave's a fine and private place,/But none, I think, do there embrace." Little did you know, Andrew Marvell, that someday, someone would come up with a charming love story, set in a graveyard, about two lost souls who are buried there, who meet and fall in love. Also inhabiting the cemetery is an eccentric old man who has the gift of being able to see and converse with the inhabitants of the graves, as well as with a raven who swoops in at mealtimes with some dinner he has swiped for the old guy. Also present from time to time is a delightful old Jewish widow, whose husband Morris is buried in the cemetery. She often stops by to tell Morris what's new. Her name is Gertrude, and it is soon apparent that she also stops by to flirt with old Jonathan Rebeck (she doesn't know he actually *lives* there). A crisis arises when it appears the young couple will be separated. The young man, it seems, has been deemed a suicide and, as such, he must be removed from consecrated ground. Their only hope is Jonathan; but to help them Jonathan must come out in the open. Had we but world enough, and time, we would tell you how Jonathan manages to salvage the romance; but we'll just have to hope the above story intrigues you enough to examine the delightful libretto and wonderfully tuneful music for yourself. A sell-out, smash hit at the Goodspeed in Connecticut and, later, at the American Stage Co. in New Jersey (the professional theatre which premiered *Other People's Money),* this happy, whimsical, sentimental, up-beat new show will delight audiences of all ages.. **(#8154)**

Other Publications for Your Interest

HOW TO EAT LIKE A CHILD
(and Other Lessons in Not Being a Grown-Up)

(ONE-ACT—MUSICAL REVUE)

By DELIA EPHRON, JOHN FORSTER
and JUDITH KAHAN

Cast of six to 30 children (10 to 15 is ideal), ages 5 to 15.
Area Staging; Unit Set

A hilarious musical romp through the joys and sorrows of being a child. A group of children gives the audience 23 "lessons" in such secret subjects as "How to Stay Home from School," "How to Beg for a Dog," "How to Torture Your Sister," "How to Act After Being Sent to Your Room," and "How to Laugh Hysterically." The pace is fast, the tone is subversive, and the recognition is instant. An added advantage: the cast size can vary from 6 children to 30 or more, depending on the size of your group. "Applause, applause, applause!"—Steve Allen. "...delightfully clever entertainment."—Hollywood Reporter. "...celebrates the spirit of youth—thanks to razzle-dazzle staging, Broadway-style songs and an imaginative script."—TV Guide. "At last a musical revue for children that can also be enjoyed by the parents...a charming and witty score..."—Backstage. "...a winner...should become a classic...It takes children's problems seriously. The result is both informational and hugely entertaining."...—Seattle Times. (Terms quoted on application. Music available on rental. See p. 195.)

(#10690)

NO MORE SECRETS

(THE MUSICAL—CHILDREN'S MUSICAL)

By GERALDINE ANN SNYDER AND PAUL LENZI

3 adults, 4 children, some doubling possible. Combination Interior-Exterior.

One of the most arresting plays for children the theatre has ever had to offer. A tense and spellbinding story on the universal theme of child abuse. On the night that her mother has night duty at the hospital, Jenny brings a friend home to spend the night. Mother has meantime asked a neighbor to keep an eye on the girls. But Jenny does not like the neighbor, or the hugs, kisses, touches and the secrets the neighbor makes Jenny keep. We see starkly the deviousness of child abusers, and how easily little children can be shamed into keeping hideous secrets. Spellbinding, with a jolting conclusion. Toured two years before publication, with sensational response.

(#16064)